#ClosingSZN

Joe Duval

#ClosingSZN
"The Young Closer's Sales Domination & Office Escape Manual for the Digital Era"

Cover Design: Joe Duval

www.joeduval.com
www.closingszn.com

Joe Duval

This book is being given as a gift to
_____ because I want to see you
accomplish your potential as a closer!

DEDICATION

This book is dedicated to Michael Daharsh, Wendey Sykora, & Sean Dwyer, and all others who lead despite a mandate to manage.

CONTENTS

An Ode to Your Greatness

An Ode to Your Greatness

The choice to be great is a simple, pragmatic decision. The choice to be average, much more irrational. It is the choice to be average that puts us at too great a risk. It is the risk of us being left to worry that we've spent too much of our lives caring about things that mattered so little, rather than pushing the boundaries of our ability off of the mental leashes to which we self-tether.

That is not to say it is easy to be great. Achieving a state of greatness must be an inherently difficult accomplishment, no matter how you choose to define it for yourself. But while reaching a state of greatness requires immense dedication, the choice to be great is far less taxing. That's because the choice to be great does not demand any sort of uncommon ability, only the development of a single habit. It is the habit of making the decision more inclined towards greatness when we are presented with a set of alternatives. Once this inclination towards greatness becomes habit, we find ourselves always walking in greener pastures. We have relieved our subconscious of average's worries by removing their manifestation from the realm of possibility.

And so, the choice to be great is not some dramatic proclamation of arrogance. It's a simple, pragmatic way of living that does well by our souls, for if the subconscious is not relieved of the worries the likes of which it's wont to marinate, it will turn against us. It will whisper things in our ear that simply aren't true. It will be emboldened to lie to us about our abilities, self-worth, and dreams. Worst of all, it will lie to us about our ability to change any and all of it by simply making one great decision. Then another.

-   Joe Duval
    Bellagio, Lago di Como, Italy
    September, 2018

1. A Note to the Young Closer

You've made a wise decision purchasing this book. I know this because, at any time I would find myself in the throes of another battle with the all-too-real phenomenon of "writer's block," I would resort back to a single question: "what would have helped *me* the most here?" In doing so I no longer had to think about all the different things I could write and was confined to only that which I myself would have found valuable as an aspiring young rainmaker.

Contrast this approach with the cacophony of sales books on the market today where the question the author seems to be asking is "how can we make this whole selling thing seem a lot easier than it really is so we can sell more books?" and you will see the reason for my confidence in deeming your purchase sage.

There are too many sales "methodology" books out there claiming that consistently closing new business can be boiled down to a set of common, finite variables shared among the prospects in our territories. The result is a lot of books sold on the promise of a shortcut that doesn't exist, and a lack of results for the would-be closer.

There are also a whole lot of books out there that seem to believe our prospective clients are the type of people that will gladly spend the precious hours of their workday answering sales-laden interrogatories about their "challenges," "business issues" and "pain points."

For those of you who have been at it a while already, how many times have we been told by sales leadership that prospects should be the ones doing most of the talking during sales interactions by asking these sorts of questions? What if they don't want to speak to us in the first place?

The reality is many of you out there have or are going to have prospects that are either averse to sales meetings altogether, or particularly averse to meeting with sales reps from your company specifically, an unfortunate situation perhaps due to the sales rep before you pounding your prospects' inboxes with so many valueless touches that you find yourself paying for the tab they drank on.

It goes without saying that hurling interrogatories at these prospects during your precious 15-30 minutes together is not a good use of their time or yours.

Because I've avoided the use of the silver bullets and selling formulas so common in other B2B sales books, you might find what I advise in these pages to require some real, honest work to implement.

The young closer rejoices in this notion.

They do so because if closing new deals with regularity were easy, everyone would be good at it and commission structures at your company would suck accordingly.

And, if selling new business were as simple as following a "selling formula," there'd be no way for you to separate yourself, financially or otherwise, and open up the doors for promotions, joint ventures, and entrepreneurial opportunities that may come your way due to your uncommon success as a young deal god.

*

This book is split into three parts, "The Sales Domination Manual," "The Mental Manual," and the "Office Escape Manual." The names I've chosen for these parts are, of course, ironic. "Manual" connotes something you can follow mindlessly without giving it any thought of your own, and if you get one thing out of this book, it's that you should only follow advice (including my own) if it comports with your own intuition and common sense. Take that which does, put it into action, and discard the rest.

Nevertheless, in combining "young closer," "sales domination," and "office escape," you can probably surmise that my goal in writing #ClosingSZN is to help young sales professionals take advantage of the incredible spoils they can generate from a career in sales and create the leverage to escape the office before inertia kicks in & we're tilling the cube-farm until the age of 65. I mean no disrespect to anyone who enjoys corporate life to this extent. It is only my own interpretation of Dante's lesser known 10th layer of Hell which has compelled me to write this book.

*

Why the "young" closer? It's not that if you don't consider yourself young you won't get anything out of all this. It is merely an indication that it is the young closer that will get the *most* out of it. That's because it is by earning more earlier in life that the young closer is set up for a remarkably quick path to financial independence, thus skipping out on the whole "I'll earn a decent salary until I'm 65 and the retire" way of thinking that depresses me to the very quick (wherever that may be).

Second, the ability to leverage your success to escape the office, travel as you'd like, and generally enjoy an unrestricted sense of freedom is something that is best experienced in our primes.

How long will it take you before you start closing more deals? Before you're able to escape the malaise of office life? That depends greatly upon the actions you take after you've finished reading. 95% of you will agree with the substance of what I've written but not actually make the changes needed to produce the results. As Americans we are obsessed with consuming; you only need to look at the number of hours we spend watching Netflix or "playing" fantasy football to see how much more we prefer it to producing.

And, although it's more heavily lauded than the forms of laze above, reading books without taking any action can quickly just become another form of consumption. Consumption doesn't ever get us paid.

If, however, you fall within the 5% of people who consistently take action upon the things you learn, you should be able to double your commissions and leverage your success to dictate when, where, and how you work within two years. This is what I was able to accomplish in my two years as a midmarket sales rep for the "End User" region at Gartner, an IT advisory firm trending towards $4B in annual revenue. These results made me Gartner's top rep two years in a row in a business unit in which most reps didn't hit quota. Many didn't make it halfway there.

The difference in results doesn't mean my peers were less talented, and they certainly weren't born out of my own innate selling ability. Indeed, when I first started selling there was a period of time I was chewed up and spit out by my prospects so thoroughly that I began to doubt my ability to ever close a single deal.

Any success I've had can instead be attributed to a continuous, exhaustive effort to figure out how I could level up from "rep" to "closer." An effort my manager Michael deemed "maniacal" in my end-of-year review following my first year on the sales floor.

This book represents an effort to distill the results of those maniacal efforts down to only the most useful insights they yielded.

*

While there are undoubtedly financial motives intertwined with the other reasons you've decided buy this book, the spoils for your efforts won't just come in the form of dollars, they will also come in the form of the leverage you'll be able to wield to begin working on your own terms, regaining control over how you spend the precious hours that make up your life.

For me this meant slinging deals while I traveled internationally, a time during which I was promoted into our large enterprise division and started earning over $200k a year before making an exit, a nest egg in tote which has enabled me to continue traveling and write this book, among other endeavors. What will it mean for you?

If you're fresh out of school or in your early 20s, imagine what your life will look like in a few years when you're 25 and have grossed over half $1M from your day job alone. You'll be on a fast track to financial freedom and location independence Tim Ferris wrote about in *The 4-Hour Workweek* without having to peddle some shit product on the internet or telling everyone you're earning exorbitant amounts of money on crypto or forex while actually living on $20 a day in Thailand

The kids you graduated school with won't know what to make of you; the world will be your oyster. Becoming an elite closer is perhaps the surest way to pull of these feats in 2019. This book will help you get there more quickly.

Welcome to #ClosingSZN.

2. A Baptism by Basic

It's the first day of your sales training academy and you're nervous and excited. Nervous because you've commenced upon the first steps of your career, and they're steps you've taken timidly. Few people go to college with *plans* to go into sales, after all. Excited because you've embarked upon a career in which you can alleviate yourself pretty quickly of the debt you've accumulated from school, and the thought of the torrent of cash you can generate from your commissions as a young rainmaker have you salivating.

You'd be a lot more nervous if your company's recruiter hadn't told you that it was OK you didn't have any sales experience prior to taking the position, and that you'd be taught everything you needed to know about closing deals from your company's sales methodology. You feel better knowing that all you'll have to do to bring in deals is follow a certain set of instructions. It makes this whole selling thing seem pretty easy, actually.

In your training academy are thirty or so new hires just like you, either brand new to sales or with little prior experience. After the first few days, your sales trainers hand out a little book with the title *"Value Selling"* across the cover.

You open your copy and see that the way to close deals is to ask your prospect questions. Lots of questions. The euphemism for these interrogations is "discovery," and its purpose is to uncover critical variables pertaining to both the prospect and their organization which, once successfully divulged from the prospect, comprise a logical basis for the prospect and their organization to want to sign an agreement for your company's product or service. These variables have names like "challenges," "business issues," and "vision of the solution."

There are also explanations of the various questioning techniques you can use to uncover these variables from the prospect with whom you meet, and you're instructed that only once you have solicited all the right information from your prospects will you be able to position your company's value proposition as the panacea to all that ails them.

"Let the prospect talk!" you are implored.

"But...what if they don't want to?" you wonder inwardly.

3. A Day in the Doldrums

March, 2015

It's 8:30 and I'm milking another few minutes in my car before I'm forced to make my way into Club Fluorescent. Things haven't been going my way, and each day that passes without a deal makes me believe a little bit more that I'm just not cut out for it. My team wheels around as I seep into my chair and I momentarily pull myself together for daps. At this point they've been the only thing that's made coming into the office bearable; the comradery is real.

After shooting the shit briefly, we abandon our desks and slide off as a group to grab breakfast from the cafeteria. At 9:30 we return just as my buddy from Finance comes over in what has become a Monday morning ritual of piecing together what happened over the weekend, each of us offering our individual moments of clarity between brownouts.

The subject of today's conversation is Friday night, when most of the sales floor was cockeyed at the bar downtown where we spend most Friday nights. It's a story with lots of elements that could make it any other weekend, with just enough nuance to prevent me from returning to the tasks at hand: the new guy getting so drunk he threw up on the bar, two reps from another team going home together, and the manager who never goes out betraying some aggressively weird dance moves to Juvenile's "Back that Ass Up."

Around 10:00 the conversation ends with the four of us bitching about Mondays. I wheel around to my desk and see the Skype for Business icon glowing in the lower righthand corner of my laptop.

It's the girl I've been seeing, and she's upset about something she heard about me over the weekend. Something that isn't true. Consumed with righteous indignation, I begin clapping back at her mistruths and soon enough I'm in a weird cyber-battle with a girl who will go on to play no major role in my life whatsoever.

It is in this manner I continue putting off the day's obligations until almost 11am, when it's time for my first meeting and ...ah, shit.

I've mixed up my meetings for the day.

I thought this morning's meeting was the throwaway I set with a tier 3 prospect just to log a meeting and satisfy my VP's mandate that all reps track and log a certain amount of meetings with new prospective clients each week.

It turns out it's not that meeting. It's actually a much more important meeting and I've done fuck all in terms of preparation. This is a "must-win" prospect, the type of prospect with lots of resources at their disposal and the type my company has had a lot of success making customers in the past.

I somewhat frantically look through my notes and try to piece together what I discussed with my prospect during the discovery meeting. It's porous at best, and the only thing I can clearly remember is her responding with agitation to all the questions I was asking, at one point responding with "they're right there on our website, Joe" when I had asked her about her company's strategic priorities for the year.

Ouch.

Wait a minute. Isn't this the deal I had gone over with my VP during a deal review? It is.

My VP, Fred, had scribbled out all the variables of the *Value Selling* "formula" on the white board to determine which of those I was missing after my discovery meeting.

He's of the opinion that, while I've done a good job getting the prospect to admit to the individual challenges she's facing in her role, I need to do a better job of uncovering how her challenges relate to her company's overall business issues and objectives for the year so I can make our service relevant to not just her, but the other stakeholders within her organization from which we'll need to gain approval before our prospect can sign.

I shift in my seat uncomfortably and tell Fred candidly that I don't think I'll be able to get any of that information given my prospect's already surly disposition towards me, and that further attempts to solicit more information will only push her away completely.

A familiar, vapid expression glazes across Fred's eyes. "Well, you've got to figure out the business issue and corporate objectives, and I'm not sure how you plan on doing that if you don't ask," he eventually offers. To drive it home, he's pointing to the whiteboard where these variables don't have anything written beside them.

The meeting with my prospect ends up going even worse than the last, as I go against all my instincts and follow Fred's advice to uncover her company's business issues by asking more questions. After cutting me short and haughtily demanding pricing, my prospect informs me she'll keep us in mind down the road should a bigger need arise to justify the cost of our services. Right.

I sit back quietly at my desk and wonder how much longer I can handle the rejection. It's been 3 months since I got on the sales floor, and I'm beginning to think I'll never close anything. I take off my headset, click out of the WebEx meeting, and start browsing Indeed.com for job openings.

Consumed with foreboding images in the not-so-distant future of everyone making fun of my broke, incapable ass, I look back over the preceding months and try to pinpoint where I had lost my way.

Then I realize I can't.

How could I have lost my way when I had never found my own way to begin with?

I stop and marinate on this question for a minute, a question the implications of which end up changing the trajectory of my sales year.

I had been blindly following the discovery-oriented tactics of *Value Selling* since I got on the sales floor. The same tactics that I had questioned back in my sales training academy. The same tactics which hadn't made sense to me form the start. Why was I continuing to follow something I didn't believe in when I wasn't seeing any results from it?

"Because everyone else does," I muse, sourly.

Could the reason I was struggling, could the reason the

whole sales floor was struggling, be because we were relying on the way we were taught to sell?

With an abundance of energy brought forth from the fear of my approaching brokeass-ness, I throw myself headfirst into trying to solve this very question.

My weekends become consumed with reading every piece of contemporary sales and business literature I can get my hands on. Things eventually get to the point where I text my manager over the weekend with ideas gleaned from my research and he replies that I need to take at least one day off per week for my sanity.

By this point, however, I'm too obsessed with figuring out how to keep prospects engaged from initial meeting to close to care about questions of sanity.

How do I take someone like the prospect I had discussed with Fred, and make her *want* to get something done with me, rather than trying to get off the phone with me as quickly as possible?

*

Fast forward to a month later and I've just closed my first deal. The next month, I close my 2nd. Then things really start heating up, and there are months where I'm closing multiple deals, culminating in a Q4 where I set a record for most new business generated by a rep in a single quarter, selling more in that quarter than my quota for the entire year.

"I have with me two gods, Persuasion and Compulsion." – Themistocles

Part I: The Sales Domination Manual

1. The Discovery Dichotomy

My quest to determine why I wasn't selling anything, and my newfound success thereafter, led me to two conclusions that stood out over any others:

ii) most of us as sales reps are reminded that we need to execute consistently, but there is little to no attention paid to what needs to go on *within* ourselves to ensure that we are consistently able to execute in the first place. The sales year is a war of mental attrition unless we have the mental model which precludes us from seeing it that way (more on this in Part II: The Mental Manual).

i) most of us as sales reps are taught to use questioning techniques all too transparently oriented towards generating value for our companies, not our prospects. Discovery-first sales methodologies don't just fail to bring any actual value to our prospects' lives, they make our prospects feel as though we're proactively detracting value form their lives for the sake of adding it to our own.

To see why this is true, we must first consider what drives human beings to make the decisions they do in the first place, in the Digital Era or any other. Then we'll look at how the time-sensitivity of the Digital Era exacerbates things.

Below is Maslow's "Hierarchy of Needs," the famous psychological theory which states that humans fulfill their needs in order of priority. The theory is often conceptualized as a pyramid:

As you travel up the pyramid, each subsequent level represents needs which you will give your attention only if your subconscious is satisfied that the needs below it are already being fulfilled. As such, "value" to human beings can be conceptualized as anything that helps us fulfill one or more of our needs without threatening our other, more important needs.

Maslow's Hierarchy is *always* at play in our lives. There is simply never a time our subconscious gives attention to higher tiers of the pyramid when our ability to satisfy the lower tiers are in serious jeopardy.

If we are out with friends and a gunman suddenly appears brandishing a weapon, our need to foster social relationships quickly takes a back seat to our much more pressing need for bodily safety. If we are in immediate danger of starving to death, we care little about our job security. In all of life's situations, therefore, the lower tiers of Maslow's hierarchy must be satisfied before our subconscious will permit us to focus on anything pertaining to higher levels of the pyramid.

And yet, Maslow's Hierarchy of Needs is incomplete and lacking mention of our most important need of all. The need that, without having in our possession, makes even food, water, and warmth irrelevant concerns. Mr. Maslow may have been taking it for granted, but the most essential human need of all is one for which we are always wishing we had more.

The most essential of all human needs is *time*.

Simply put, if we don't have any time (left), we've by some way or another reached the end of our lives, and at that point *none* of the other tiers of Maslow's pyramid have any importance at all.

This is why we find ourselves thinking about the passage of time so often; it's our most important need and it's the only one for which we have a finite, depleting supply.

Now that we're fully immersed in the Digital Era, time has taken up its rightful place at the bottom of the pyramid, and the need for (*more*) *time* has taken up permanent residence in our collective mindshare.

Why?

Reading this likely means that you live in the industrialized world and your subconscious has the luxury of taking the traditional base layer of Maslow's pyramid – physiological needs like food, water, and warmth – for granted. I for once

17

don't ever wake up consumed with whether or not I'm going to be able to eat that day, or if I will be sufficiently clothed such that I don't succumb to the elements.

We never think about these things, yet most of us ponder our mortality regularly and live in existential angst about whether or not we're making the best use of the time we have on earth.

Put differently, while Ötzi the Iceman spent a lot of time thinking about attacks from wild animals and the prospect of freezing to death, our minds are more consumed with the approaching passage of another birthday.

An updated hierarchy of needs thus looks something more like this:

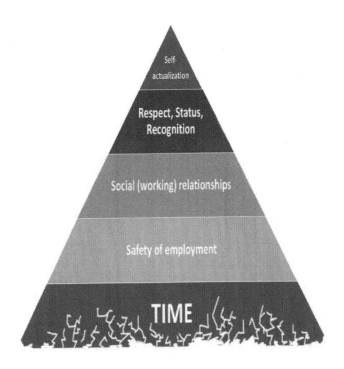

The ever-increasing value humans are placing on their time is not lost on the world's most innovative business leaders and entrepreneurs, many of whom are putting time-value at the forefront of their company's value proposition.

Jeff Bezos' entire corporate strategy for Amazon hinges on wasting as little of, and giving as much as possible in return for, the customer's time during each interaction that person has on the Amazon web portal.

Because of this focus, Amazon is able to help us find the products we want with blazing efficiency. By synthesizing vast amounts of data into meaningful insights, Amazon's algorithms are also able to make product recommendations that complement the ones for which we originally searched. These recommendations have the power to save us the time we'd spend at some point down the road once we realize we needed the additional items too. Checkout happens with as little as one click of the mouse, and you'll have the items you ordered within two days, one day, or even on the very same day as your order.

Bruh, have you ever had same-day delivery from Amazon before? It's a sliver of heaven on this time-bound earth. A sliver brought to your very doorstep. Within hours. Bruh.

By focusing on time-value Amazon has taken the negative thoughts we associate with *having* to spend our time at the store – and hoping we go to the one with the item we want in stock, that we won't overpay for it, that we won't have to make another trip to return it, that we won't get stuck in traffic, that we won't have to stop for gas – with the joy of getting exactly what we want while spending as little of our most precious and perpetually depleting need as possible.

The immense value we rightly place on our time as our most important need cannot be underestimated by the aspiring closer, and it is here where selling methodologies like Value Selling, Solution Selling, and the bevy of other discovery/question-based selling frameworks out there get everything wrong.

These methodologies treat our prospect's time as if it were their least valuable asset instead of their most coveted need!

After all, who has really gotten something for their 30 minutes at the conclusion of a discovery meeting?

Your prospect, who is told that during the *next* meeting you'll be able to show them how your company might be able to help them via a product demo or services overview?

Or you, who now has a war chest full of sales ammo to lord over them when they end up not wanting to sign your agreement via poignantly placed yet ultimately ineffective "FUD" bombs? "But you said you're spending $100k a year on services you could cut out if you went with us, what do you mean we're too expensive!?"

*

Does the ever-increasing value we're putting on our time thus put the would-be closer in an impossible position? How are we to deliver more time-value during our interactions with prospects? After all, we're not a bunch of Amazonian algorithms that can get our prospects exactly what they need in nanoseconds, and B2B transactions are much more complicated than B2C transactions – the products and services cost more money, multiple stakeholders are involved in the purchasing decision, and a lot of people might stand to be affected by a decision to move forward.

Let's not miss the forest for the trees. The takeaway from all this isn't necessarily *how* Amazon gives us more value for our time (i.e. by getting us from start to finish as quickly and seamlessly as possible), it's that the value we find in Amazon's buying experience is becoming the primary reason we choose to buy from Amazon over other companies in the first place.

And, because as closers *we* are the buying experience, the practical implication is that you, yourself are becoming more and more likely to be the primary reason your prospect ends up doing business with your company over your company's competitors. Just because you cannot give prospects back more of their time in the way an Amazon can, doesn't mean you can't give them more value for the time they *do* spend with you.

The result is a psychological inclination to want to get something done with you (and your company) over reps who do not, or cannot, value their time to this extent.

In terms of the actions needed to right the ship, closers need to shift the focus from the value the prospect and their company would ultimately gain from our company's product or service, to first ensuring that the prospect feels as though they are getting value from the time they spend with us during each and every interaction leading up to close.

It's less about finding additional areas where your company adds value to your prospect's challenges and priorities *if they were to become a client* and more about finding ways to help during the 15, 30, or 60 minutes we have with the prospect *right now*. It's less about "value-added sales," and more about an evolution into the "value-adding salesperson."

All this isn't to say, of course, that you can get by without having a thorough understanding of how your company's product/service would benefit the prospect if they were actually to become a customer. I'm taking it for granted you have a clear understanding of your company's value proposition.

But in order for your prospect to fully commit to evaluating that value proposition, and the multitude of meetings and logistical headaches that might go along with it, they're first going to have to be sold on the idea of spending so much time *with you*. The closer's very first objective, therefore, is to begin getting them to feel this way as quickly as possible.

Nor does this mean there is no more room for asking your prospect great questions. But those questions need to be just that, great, and asked when you've already begun to establish in the mind of the prospect that you are the type of person who's worth their time. By doing so, the odds of you actually getting useful answers to any questions you ask increase dramatically.

After all, who's going to get more meaningful information from a prospect? The closer who has identified an opportunity to provide value to a prospect and from the outset starts working to deliver it? Or the sales rep who first informs the prospect "I'll be the one asking the questions here!" before displaying any sort of individual competence, willingness, or ability to actually help with anything at all?

In fact, if you focus on providing more value to your prospects during each interaction you have with them, you may find that you need to ask fewer questions in the first place, as your prospects start to divulge helpful information on their own. This is a clear-cut sign that you've won or on your way to winning the 1st Sale, as outlined in the chapters that make up the Sales Domination Manual.

A final word on digital's impact on your prospects. As we venture further into the Digital Era, your prospects adverse reactions to spending time providing you and your company information via stereotypical, value-detracting discovery meetings is only going to become more pronounced. Do yourself a favor and reorient your mindset to the Digital Era *now* and you'll have taken your first step from "sales rep" to "closer."

2. Introduction to the 1st Sale

In light of the buying expectations of the Digital Era, we have re-prioritized "value" to emphasize the value which you, personally, are able to provide prospects for their time during each and every interaction you have with them such that you yourself become the competitive differentiator separating your company from its competitors in the mind of your prospect.

We are less focused at the outset of our interactions on making a value-based sale, and more focused on becoming a value-adding salesperson. Our ability to provide value to our prospects during each and every interaction is the B2B equivalent of the value-added buying experiences becoming ubiquitous in the B2C arena, not in terms of time returned back to our prospects, but in terms of our prospects getting more value for that time, their most important need.

This is what makes our prospect inclined to *want* to get something accomplished with us, which is the first of two sales we'll have to make in order to close the deal (the 2nd is them getting approval and/or consensus for moving forward with the deal internally).

People still buy form people, and there is a tendency to believe that the people that are bought from the most simply have more innate "sales DNA" than everyone else. If true, it's only because these individuals have a more intuitive understanding of what needs to happen in the mind of their prospect for that prospect to be sold on spending their time coming over to our side of the table and start selling *with* us instead of being sold to.

We can conceptualize what happens in the mind of the prospect when the closer reaches this point as the successful activation of a series of "Mental Triggers" within your prospect's subconscious which, once activated, result in your prospect's psychological inclination towards trying to get a deal accomplished with you over the litany of other reps selling similar products and services, as well as all the other things the prospect could spend their time on that have nothing to do with taking a sales meeting at all (i.e. the status quo):

1. Compelling Relevance
2. Authority
3. Consistency
4. Reciprocity
5. Trust & Liking

For the most part, these mental triggers have little to do with your company's product or service, and everything to do with you.

3. Mental Trigger 1 – Compelling Relevance

"To be persuasive we must be believable; to be believable we must be credible; credible we must be truthful" – Edward Murrow

A popular refrain among corporate sales methodologies is to "diagnose before you prescribe," meaning that you should make sure you understand the prospect's challenges before recommending a solution. This is the proposed basis for asking so many questions during discovery meetings.

It sounds benign enough at first. After all, we expect our doctor to ask us a series of questions to determine what's wrong with us rather than assuming they know from our outward symptoms alone and prescribing something that may or may not do us any good.

There's a big difference, however, between your doctor asking you questions to understand what's wrong and you

25

doing the same with your prospects during a sales meeting. For one, there isn't any way for your doctor to figure out what might be wrong with you ahead of time by hopping on the internet and forming a hypothesis from all the information about you available online that points her in the right direction even before we open our sickly mouths to tell her.

This is not the case for the business executives to whom most of us sell. For these individuals and their businesses, there is no shortage of information out there we can gather ahead of time – from annual reports, company newsletters, stated corporate objectives, forward looking statements, Google News, LinkedIn, and on and on – to make a compelling case for how our product or service could help fix a challenge without having to put them through a full-blown interrogation first.

Moreover, remember that it is you that seeks the assistance of a doctor, not the other way around. As closers the reality is most of our prospects haven't sought us out and aren't exactly jumping at the idea of meeting with us. Most sales methodologies conveniently ignore this reality.

Chances are, in fact, that you're going to have a lot of prospects that give you one chance at being compellingly relevant enough to their interests to agree to meet with you again for more substantive conversations. In my experience there are more than a handful of C-Level executives that will tell you so much explicitly, to the effect of "I have 15 minutes for you Joe, show me what you've got."

The *last* thing you want to do in a situation with one of these prospects is fuck it up by asking them the same basic discovery-oriented questions they get asked by the dozens of other sales reps flooding their inboxes with generic sales spam every day. This is exactly how you tell your prospect's subconscious that you are the same sort of value-detracting sales rep to which they've become accustomed and the reason for which they are being so guarded with their time in the first place; the type the prospect has met with so often only to find the meeting a complete waste of time and the rep incapable of helping them actually accomplish anything.

The result is that rather than give you any meaningful answers to your questions, they'll be thinking about how they can get off the phone with you as quickly as possible instead.

*

The first thing your prospect's subconscious wants to see from you instead during this crucial introductory window is that you and what you're positioning are relevant enough to their interests for you to warrant more of their time.

On the surface, delivering a relevant message that constitutes a basis for a meeting and the ones to follow shouldn't be difficult for even the average rep upon whom we would never bestow the title of "closer."

Where the average rep often falls short, however, is having a deep enough understanding of how the prospect views their world so as not only propose a meeting relevant and tailored to the prospect's interest, but compellingly so.

Reaching a compelling level of relevance in the mind of your prospect requires a genuine understanding of your prospect's situation, and this in turn requires a higher than expected level of expertise into your prospect's world. Consider that *The Challenger Sale* beseeches sales reps to focus on "commercial teaching," whereby reps deliver insights to their clients so valuable that they are actually enabling that client's organization to compete more effectively in their market.

This is an incredibly lofty standard for the aspiring young closer who often has a couple decades of experience less than the prospect to whom they are selling, but it is absolutely the one to which you should aspire, because anything less can signal to your prospects subconscious that you don't "get it," and spending time with a person that doesn't get it is just a waste of that time. This is particularly true for the C-level and senior business executives to whom most of us sell.

In the same vein, Neil Rackham is famous for urging sales professionals to make their sales meetings so valuable that their customers would pay for the conversations themselves.

It requires an extraordinary amount of understanding into your prospect's world to be able to deliver this kind of value in exchange for your prospect's time, and accumulating this level of expertise appears a herculean effort when you're just starting out as a rep in your given industry.

There's no substitute for doing the work. You must simply do the research, and more importantly, you must actually turn that knowledge gained from your research into muscle memory such that you don't have to rely upon "talk tracks' during your meetings with prospects.

Talk tracks are insufficient in becoming compelling relevant to your prospect because relying upon them means you lack the ability to add value to the conversation when it inevitably flows to a point outside of that particular track, where your expertise ends.

As soon as your prospect asks a question that demands more explanation from you, or objects to something you've said, you won't be able to contend. You must therefore have a holistic understanding of your prospect's world to get to the level we're alluding to here. It's this level of expertise which enables you to stop relying upon discovery questions intended to get the prospect to connect the dots for you and enables you to begin connecting the dots for them instead.

The good news is that learning a lot of potentially dense, potentially less-than-exciting material pertaining to your prospect's world is easier than you think once you make an upgrade to the way you learn and retain information.

In high school and college most of our learning efforts involved memorizing facts and concepts then regurgitating them during an exam in our fanciest prose (particularly true for us liberal arts majors). The way we memorized these concepts usually involved some form of repetition, like flash cards.

It was by sheer osmosis, then, that a lot of us succeeded in keeping information fresh in our noodles long enough to pass our exams, at which point we'd forget all the shit we just "learned" and start focusing on information for the next one. Rinse and repeat.

Those habits have carried over from our formal education into our careers. The problem is exacerbated, however, because we don't' have the structure of classes to ensure we at least regularly expose ourselves to the right information. Instead, our learning practices as dealmakers typically devolve into something like reading a couple industry-related posts on LinkedIn when we don't feel like making prospect calls.

All we can hope for from this type of "learning" is that every now and then something of relevance will randomly bubble up from the recesses of our brain-pieces that impresses our prospect during a meeting. That rarely works, and the result is that we revert back to the same tired-ass questions and talk tracks we've relied upon so ineffectively to this point.

As such, there are really two obstacles for aspiring closers to overcome in the quest to become compellingly relevant to their prospects: 1) inconsistency and information overload, and 2) ineffective learning.

Inconsistency and Information Overload

If you're only boning up on your industry, business, and prospect-related acumen when you feel like it (that is, very rarely), your brain will just shove it out of focus as soon as you stop reading and replace it with whatever stimuli you normally spend your time ingesting.

This is mostly a quantitative issue, and in that sense your brain resembles a computer. A computer as a maximum storage capacity (say a 500GB hard drive), the accessibility of which is limited by its active memory (RAM, say 16GB). That 16GB represents all the information your computer can recall at any given point in time, which is why there's a limit to the number of programs your computer can run at once.

Following the analogy, the relevant pieces of information in which you ask your brain to recall and apply in a given situation are like the programs on your computer in that you are limited in how much information you can recall and use at any given point in time.

Thus, the more you're focused on filler, the less you will be able to recall the information that's most compelling to your prospects because your brain's active memory is already occupied with other bullshit. The problem is one of information overload, and it's becoming more and more prevalent as the sheer amount of information to which we're exposed on a daily basis continues to proliferate through digital mediums like social media at an exponential rate.

To become a closer, therefore, you must not only be more consistent in your uptake of information of compelling relevance to your prospects, you also need to be more selective of the other information you choose to consume.

You must reorient yourself from information overload to information mastery by cutting out a lot of the filler and habitually ingesting the right information instead. For example, instead of taking 30 minutes every morning before work on Reddit, use those 30 minutes to explore what's trending in importance in the world in which your prospect inhabits.

If this is too much for you to take, if you can't cut down on the Netflix binges to gain the knowledge you need to succeed to consistently come off as relevant to your prospect's interests, then you may do well to consider changing careers now, because you'll never become a closer and sales is too stressful a career to justify becoming anything less.

Are the activities you engage in on a daily & nightly basis really worth trading 40 years of your life and retiring when you're 65? Or would it be better if you put a lot of that shit to the side for the next 2-3 years and get one foot out of the rat race while you're still in your prime?

Make no mistake, a lot of your friends might find it odd when you start spending less time hanging and more time working, and that's a scary thought, but I'm not one of those meatwads on YouTube yelling at you to cut your friends out of your life because "they don't believe in you." That's a misguided attempt to blame others for our own inability to block out the noise. Your friends will naturally be skeptical when you suddenly start acting like the Kobe of the sales game. Take it as your moral obligation to endure any incredulous or potentially negative reactions so that you may not only accomplish what you set out to accomplish for yourself, but perhaps motivate some of them to do the same along the way.

Remember, none of your friends understand how badly you want to succeed like you do. None of them have seen the amount of thought you've put into "sacrificing" a lot of the activities in which you currently partake to obtain a standard of living beyond that which is normal. None of them have been privy to the nights you've spent imagining all the things you're going to do once you pop. If they had, they'd more readily accept the forthcoming changes, but instead all they really see is the part where you say "I'm going to be hanging out less and working more." Their reaction is natural, so don't cut them out, endure and inspire them instead.

Now that we have gotten it out of the way that becoming a modern day deity of persuasion and compulsion will in fact take some sacrifice, let's look at how you can get a lot more bang for your buck when giving yourself the education necessary to become compellingly relevant in the mind of your prospect.

Ineffective Learning

If becoming more consistent and selective in the type of information we choose to consume is what enables us to become compellingly relevant in the minds of our prospects, developing stronger neural connections around that information is how we are able to get to that point much more quickly.

Recall the remarkably ineffective ways we've become used to learning information: either the bare bones "read and hope it sticks" method or memorization through repetition. We must abandon these learning habits and commit to a way of learning that enables the information we need to be more easily recalled when it would be useful during a prospect meeting.

Humans are highly emotional creatures, and words in and of themselves carry very little emotional weight. This is a problem because things that carry little emotional weight tend not to stick around in our minds for very long. In fact, when we find words to be emotionally charged it is because the author has been effective in conjuring up dramatic imagery in our minds; it is the images and feelings the words evoke that make them memorable, not the words themselves.

And, because the information we need to learn to be compellingly relevant to our prospects usually isn't emotionally charged in an inherent sense (i.e. it's dry), it makes sense that to learn key concepts more effectively we should translate those concepts from words to images to make them more recallable when we're meeting with our prospects.

The below is a memory technique I've used with success in this regard, and one that many memory experts recommend to improve our ability to recall relevant information when needed.

It is the technique that in many ways mimics how people with "photographic" memories naturally remember things. It involves making cognitive impressions (images) of key concepts and linking these images with one another through narrative, so that you only need to remember one image to remember all the images that make up the "scene."

What you'll end up doing is not only creating a series of highly memorable images that represent the key ideas/concepts that relate to your prospect's world, but through the story that connects them you'll understand how these images (ideas/concepts) relate to other images (ideas/concepts) in the "scene" (the aggregate of all the ideas/concepts you're trying to remember).

Below is an example of how I might use this technique on an a piece of research if I were a closer selling Agile and DevOps management software to Chief Information Officers in the banking industry:

*"For several years banks have been seeing **IT failures** coming from **Agile and DevOps** in core banking systems. These systems play vital roles in the performance of the core IT infrastructure that make banking processes otherwise run smoothly.*

Before the proliferation of technology began complicating the tech ecosystem on which these banks rely, a developer could take system-wide ramifications into account before *writing code. **However, with the increased usage of methodologies such as agile, developers are not entirely aware of the effects that which they are building will render in real time.** This is because there is no basis to view the changes set to take place in the banking system before it is set to go live. The result is that Agile is destabilizing the design process and DevOps is corroding the "go live" procedures which had previously made sure everything would go off without a hitch before launch.*

*Due to these reasons, it wouldn't be wrong saying that archaic methodologies were cheaper than Agile and DevOps, and **many banking professionals believe legacy systems to perform more satisfactorily.***"

The words in bold are the concepts for which I'll create mental images. The images we use to represent concepts should be 1) the first thing that springs to mind and 2) made extra ridiculous. They will be linked together naturally through the events of what we've just read:

Concept/Idea	Mental Image Associated
1. IT Failures	Computers flashing "ALERT" on them and catching on fire, like a nuclear meltdown
2. Agile & Dev Ops	Navy Seals ("ops") flipping, somersaulting, jumping through the air between computers melting down ("agile")
3. Developers not completely aware of what they're building	Stevie Wonder typing in random letters of code on a keyboard with a shit-eating grin on his face while the computers are melting down and the Navy Seals are flipping all around him

4. Professional bankers believing legacy systems were better	In the midst of all this madness a rich old banker resembling the Monopoly Man hugging one of those enormous IBM mainframes from back when computers were first invented

First, it's important to note that I've used concrete objects from the text to outline what I think are the article's main ideas, or the ideas that I otherwise deem worthy of remembering in relation to what I already know about my prototypical prospect. It's best that you build your images around objects (nouns) rather than verbs or adjectives which aren't as easily translated to imagery on their own ("cat" prompts the image of a cat to appear in your mind's eye, whereas "fast" prompts the image of...?).

I then associate vivid imagery with the concepts I've chosen. For example , "IT failures" turns into a nuclear meltdown. What happens during this nuclear meltdown? The Navy Seals (dev "ops") bust in to help resolve the situation, with all of their agility ("agile") on full display.

And then what? As the Navy Seals are running around trying to figure out how to stop the meltdown, we see Stevie Wonder attempting to code (Stevie Wonder is blind, so that obviously isn't going great). Finally, the scene cuts to the Monopoly Man (a banking professional, in this case) hugging an old IBM mainframe (one of those ones from the 80's...a legacy system) which has served him so well in the past.

The uptick of creating a dramatic scene from these otherwise unmemorable and dry ideas is that we now have a memorable series of images we won't forget if for nothing else but that they're so inane.

As such, when we're on the phone with our prospects discussing how our software can help agile developers see the effects they are rendering more clearly in real time, we are able to extract relevant information from a scene that is already vividly engrained in our minds rather than hoping the concepts, dull in-and-of-themselves due to a lack of emotional intrigue, have stuck around in our head.

In learning information that pertains to our prospects' everyday reality in such a way, by *imprinting* that information into our heads in the form of an image, over time we are able to achieve a much more intimate level of understanding of our prospects and the worlds they inhabit we otherwise wouldn't have. We have improved our ability to become compellingly relevant to our prospects because we understand their world at a much more empathetic level.

How does this play out? Well, if I'm selling computer software to CIOs that enables their programmers using agile and DevOps methodologies to better see the effects of what they're building in real time, I'm able to riff with my prospect about Stevie Wonder trying to program, or their banker colleagues who, like the Monopoly Man pining for the days of old, are confused as to why the bank is implementing these programming methodologies in the first palace when the old systems seemed perfectly satisfactory.

What I'm really conveying is an empathetic understanding of the situation to my prospect's subconscious, and empathy is compellingly relevant because it shows your prospects that you are one of those rare sales reps that actually "gets it." Reps that "get it" are the ones that get more time on the calendar, and reps that get more time on the calendar are reps that ultimately put themselves in a position to close.

*

As mentioned, the images you associate with what you feel are important concepts should generally be those that first come to mind. This is important. You don't want to fight against what you're naturally inclined to use as imagery. You want your mind to default to the images you create as naturally as possible.

Once these images pop into your head, you should then make them a little more ridiculous. For example, Stevie Wonder trying to code is already memorable, but that I've made the image more ridiculous by having him have a shit-eating grin on his face while making the world around him burn cements the image in my memory, making it easily recallable should I want to use the concept of programmers having no idea what they're coding during a prospect conversation.

The beauty of this method is trifold:

1) First, in learning ideas and concepts pertaining to our prospect's world in such a manner, I don't actually need to try to "remember" anything while on the phone or across the table from my prospect when discussing these topics. The images are already there to tell us, passively, because I had actively stored them there when learning the material. Contrast this with learning ideas and concepts via the "read it and hope it sticks" method which constitutes passive learning. In these instances we haven't stored anything to represent the concepts/ideas we want to remember, so that when we're on the phone with our prospect we have to *try* to remember what those words and ideas mean to the prospect with nothing there to give us any indication:

Passive Learning (read it and hope it sticks)	Leads to	Active recollection- trying to remember what the ideas and concepts we had previously learned mean to the prospect because we have nothing there to make sense of them other than the words themselves
Active Learning	Leads to	Passive recollection -not needing to try to remember what the ideas and concepts we had previously learned mean to the prospect because we already have images there to make sense of them, along with a narrative that tells us how the ideas/concepts relate to one another

Passive learning leads to active recollection. Active learning leads to passive recollection

2) Even if we don't store every idea/concept we're trying to remember with strong enough imagery to make the recollection of those concepts passive, just the act of attempting to do so will help us remember much more relevant information than if we had just read it and hoped to be able to recall the information through osmosis.

3) Most importantly, when developing the subject matter expertise necessary to become compellingly relevant to your prospects, to have conversations with your prospects which enable them to compete more effectively in their market (*Challenger Sale*) and which are so valuable they would be willing to pay for them (Neil Rackham), you'll be able to drastically reduce the learning curve it takes to this point.

You'll be able to skim lengthy, potentially boring subject matter and create images to remember the important concepts. This will enable you to be able to recall them naturally when applicable to the conversation at hand with your prospect, as your prospect merely mentioning "DevOps" will cause the previously stored images to pop into your mind, along with the narrative which tells you how the concepts the images represent relate to one another, whereas the mention of "DevOps" would have previously prompted nothing to pop into your mind besides the word itself.

For more on this particular learning technique, I suggest reviewing *The Memory Book: The Classic Guide to Improving Memory at Work, at School, and at Play* from which it is derived.

Whether this learning technique or another, you must go about your uptake of information more strategically than the passive learning to which you've become accustomed.

Passive learning signifies reading each article and hoping things stick, and they won't unless you're able to invest hours upon hours (upon hours) into reading and re-reading the same subject matter.

The risk here is that it takes you too far into your sales year to gain the level of expertise that would otherwise permit you to be compelling relevant to your prospects such that you succumb to selling like everyone else due to the sheer pressure that comes with a few months going by and having nothing to show for them, or the work entailed appearing so colossal that you say "fuck it" before you can begin to reap that which you've sown.

*

In any case, now that we've 1) consistently (every morning/afternoon/evening/whatever) and 2) effectively (through active learning) begun to accumulate the expertise we need to be compellingly relevant to the interests of our prospect, we will feel less need to rely upon the "talk tracks" and discovery-oriented tactics which tell your prospect's subconscious, "hey, do you mind if I use 30 minutes of your time to figure out how I'm supposed to sell you something?"

It's an empowering advantage knowing that you hold a prospect's interest and attention without having to rely upon them to tell you what ails them first. Your prospect's subconscious will appreciate how deftly you're able to cut to the chase, associating you as the rep that should get their time over all the others that can't bring anything to the table themselves.

Compelling Relevance is one half of what gets you past the initial "waste of time or nah" filtering system of your prospect's subconscious during your initial interaction with them, and what eventually translates into your prospect saying "yea, let's go ahead and schedule another 30 minutes to flesh this out more." The other half of this filter has nothing to do with what you're able to say, and everything to do with how you say it.

4. Mental Trigger 2 – Authority

"Character may almost be called the most effective means of persuasion." – Aristotle

The 2nd half of getting past the "waste of time or nah" filter in your prospect's subconscious is the Authority Trigger. Establishing the Authority Trigger tells your prospect's subconscious "I am the type of person with whom you should associate, and because of that, I am worth your time."

Its effectiveness lies in the human need, rooted deep within our ancestral DNA, to spend our time associating with the "right" people in order to survive.

Establishing the Authority Trigger is the product of the tone (the overall attitude your voice conveys), intonation (the fluctuation of that tone), and when applicable, your body language.

In a typical sales meeting by phone/teleconference, the Authority Trigger is in play as soon as the sound waves emitting from your voice have reached your prospect's receiver.

Why is this so important?

Recall our homie, Maslow. Security of employment & working (social) relationships are important needs to humans. Your prospect does not want to risk going to bat for your service or putting you in front of their peers & superiors if they think there's a chance that you're the type of person with whom associating might make them look bad. Doing so would pose a risk to those needs. Authority is the Mental Trigger which soothes this worry and tells them that's not the case.

So how do you convey it?

*

Say it with your Chest, but Smartly

Sales organizations are replete with sales leaders imploring their reps to speak with more "conviction" when working with prospects, but all "conviction" really means is speaking in a manner which conveys you strongly believe that which you're claiming.

Is it good to sound convicted when what you're saying is laughably inaccurate? No, that just makes you a blowhard, not a closer.

This is why you want to speak in a manner that conveys authority instead. "Authority" suggests there is finality on the matter, and that the listener should be inclined to defer to that which is said on the basis of who's saying it. It suggests to your prospect's subconscious that the prospect should be inclined to believe what you're saying because you don't sound like the you'd be the type of person that would be wrong about it. This is how you want to speak, as it will get your prospect's subconscious to start whispering "I think she's right."

Not only do most sales organizations neglect teaching their reps how to speak with more authority as part of their routine sales training, for whatever reason there is a tendency to believe traits like these can't be taught at all. Consider what the authors of *The Challenger Sale* believe about "charisma," for example.

In that work, the authors state explicitly that while traits like "charisma" might be hugely important to sales success, they did not include them in their analysis of what makes sales reps successful because they want to enable sales leaders to achieve success with the reps they *already have*.

Notice what the authors are actually saying here. They're saying that if a rep currently doesn't come off a particular way (in their example, charismatically, in ours, authoritatively), there's nothing to be done about it.

That would be a big problem if it were true, as anyone that's been in the game for any period of time knows how important it is to bring a certain juice to a sales meeting in order for it to go well. Fortunately, it's an assumption that isn't based in reality, and there are several things we can do in order to improve our ability to establish the authority with which we speak to our prospects.

First, the ability to speak with authority (or conviction or charisma for that matter) increases dramatically as our subject matter expertise improves. We naturally convey that our assertations should be taken as correct when we know with certainty that they *are* correct.

This is why Authority follows Compelling Relevance as the 2nd Mental Trigger. While the two are established in tandem in the mind of your prospect, the active learning which enables you to become compellingly relevant to your prospects' interests will automatically compel you to speak with more authority on those interests as well.

The second is the **elimination of verbal tics**. Think back to college and a professor that you found particularly persuasive. A person whose word was never doubted in relation to their chosen field of expertise. Did that person convey ideas through a muddled confluence of "uh's," "you know's" and "kind of's"? A rhetorical question, of course.

One of my former VPs would, while leading meetings attended by dozens of reps, repeatedly insert a "you know?" at the end of every other sentence.

What this really conveys to the listener is that it's *you* that doesn't know, and that you're asking permission that being in the general ballpark is good enough. You're asking, "hey man, I know I might not entirely be on the spot here, but I'm close enough, right?" No, you're not. Not when you're asking for that person's time to consider an offer you've portrayed as compelling to their interests. You need to know damn well what that offer entails and why it's so compelling, and you need to sound like that's the case to prevent your prospect's subconscious from yelling "Great! Just what we need! Another sales wankster wasting our time over something they don't even understand!"

Then there are enunciation, vocabulary, and pace:

Enunciation – If you tend to mumble, or otherwise lack a crispness in your diction, you must practice speaking with more clarity. It is proper enunciation which enables us to speak with exactitude, and speaking with exactitude conveys a calm belief in the words we are speaking due to its effect on pace, as explained below.

Vocabulary – I don't mean dropping as many $10-word bombs on your prospect as you can, but rather your ability to speak with the same vernacular when needed. You must be able to use business and industry-specific words in situations where an industry professional would be expected to use them.

For example, if you're a sales rep for a company that sells cloud infrastructure, but don't ever distinguish between public, private, and hybrid cloud environments (perhaps referring to all of it simply as "the cloud" instead), the subconscious of the director of infrastructure to whom you're selling is going to have a hard time seeing you as the type of person whose word we should take for granted on the matter.

Pace – speaking too quickly has the tendency to make us look nervous – the "fast-talking" salesman talking hurriedly in the hopes that we'll miss the finer points of his bullshit. You don't want to be associated with that guy. You also don't want to slow things down too much, because then you'll just appear, uh, slow. "Non-hurried but deliberate" is the best way to describe the pace you're looking for in order to avoid being put in either one of these baskets.

*

One way to work on our ability to establish the Authority Trigger is to record ourselves pitching. Listen for weaknesses. Do you intuitively sound convincing? Do you sound natural using the industry-specific words your prospects use daily? Are there any verbal tics that might cue your prospect's subconscious into thinking "this guy's full of shit."?

Of course, this is something you'd benefit from doing with a manager or teammate if they're receptive to it, but if they're not, don't use it as an excuse not to improve. Grab your iPhone, hit the record button, and embrace the awkwardness of delivering the world's greatest sales pitch to yourself. You'll feel stupid at first, but you'll be grateful once you start to hear the power in your words. It's an amazing feeling to deliver a pitch with enough authority that you know your prospect has bitten before they can utter a word in response. *Steph Curry with the shot, boi.*

5. Mental Trigger 3 - Consistency

"Consistency is the true foundation of trust. Either keep your promises or do not make them." – Roy T. Bennett

Consistency has been a long-valued character trait in all societies, and inconsistent individuals are generally regarded as untrustworthy and unreliable. During the bloodbaths of election season, what is always one of the top criticisms political rivals hurl against one another?

"First she said X, but then she did Y."

"The mayor promised during his past campaign to do X, Y, and Z if elected, and he hasn't done any of them! Does he really deserve reelection?"

In our own workplaces, consistency is what gets people promoted, and lack of consistency, fired. If you've worked in a corporate environment for any period of time, you've likely seen how consistency beats out talent when executive management stocks the senior leadership ranks with individuals who, while never having incredible performances as individual sales contributors, have shown a remarkable consistency in their dedication to the company.

We associate consistency with professionalism. Think about it. What do we say when someone has a remarkably consistent track record of getting things accomplished?

"That guy's a pro."

In our context as closers, consistency tells your prospect's subconscious you are the type of professional that will bring value to *every* interaction required to get the deal done, including interactions where your prospect might stick out their neck by bringing their colleagues (and thus their colleague's time) to the table.

This is vitally important. Why?

Well, let's think back to our homie Maslow and the Hierarchy of Needs. If you look at the pyramid, you'll notice that the majority of human needs have a social element attached to them in which inconsistency poses a threat.

For example, being inconsistent at work means we'll have a hard time holding down a job (safety of employment). Inconsistency also threatens our ability to have quality relationships (working or otherwise) because others can't depend on us. Finally, it damages our ability to garner respect/status/recognition, all of which depend on the social standing which inconsistency has the power to erode. As such, we do whatever we can not to appear inconsistent in our professional lives, *including not associating with inconsistent people.*

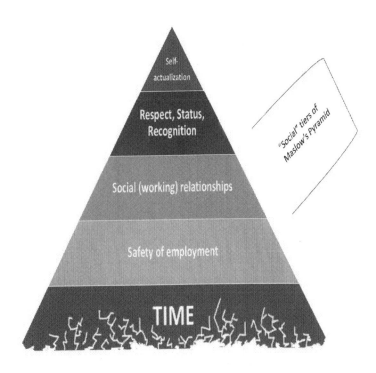

For closers, activating the Consistency Trigger in the mind of your prospect entails:

1. Delivering value during *every* prospect-facing meeting such that 1) your prospect begins associating your consistency with the consistency of your company's overall value proposition and 2) your prospect doesn't worry that you might make them look foolish if other stakeholders from their organization need be brought to your meetings

2. Following through on *every* post-meeting action item you discuss with your prospect when you say you're going to do them, or before you say you're going to do them

3. Holding firm around messaging pertaining to why your prospect & their organization should become clients, and not flipping to another angle as soon as you start getting push back. The latter is often a buying tactic intended to test your belief in that which you're proposing. Consistency reinforces your belief in the value proposition of your product or service while quickly switching to highlight another erodes it.

Remember that before they become a customer, the association your prospect has of your company and the product or service it provides is completely enveloped in you. If you're inconsistent with the value you're bringing to the table, your prospect is liable to start associating your own inconsistency with the inconsistency of your company's product or service.

6. Mental Trigger 4 - Reciprocity

"The value of a man resides in what he gives and not in what he is capable of receiving." – Albert Einstein

The Reciprocity Trigger is my favorite of the Mental Triggers because its activation represents the point where your prospect begins accomplishing tasks designed to move the deal forward with a vigor much more equal to your own. I also like it because your prospect's need to reciprocate accumulates in proportion to the value you are able to deliver throughout the sales cycle, such that the more value you are able to deliver to your prospect over time, the more your prospect will feel an obligation to return your efforts.

The urge to reciprocate becomes especially intense when you're near the end of a sales cycle and your prospect begins asking *you* for additional time in helping them get internal approval for your company's product or service:

"Hey, I think the executive summary you sent over is good, but could you make the outlined changes? I think it will resonate more with the CEO."

"I think what would be best is if you came on site and met with our CFO and his team to explain some of these things. Do you think you'd be able to do that next week?"

"Legal is requesting we put an NDA in place before we talk any further. Is that something you can get accomplished on your end?"

With all of these requests, your prospect, who by this point is sold on what your company is going to provide but does not yet have the requisite approvals, is asking for a lot of time from you. Their subconscious will urge them to put their best foot forward in getting the deal accomplished internally or risk the perceived social ramifications of taking so much of your time without giving what is expected in return. At some point, "what is expected in return" becomes a signed agreement.

The Reciprocity Trigger is partly a by-product of the Consistency Trigger, as your prospect's subconscious will not only want them to reciprocate the effort you've expended bringing value to their interests, but also your ability to be so predictable in doing so. Nevertheless, we can get more out of the Reciprocity Trigger by looking for ways to provide value to our prospects which are unique to them.

It is our ability to help our prospects in ways which they feel are 1) genuinely helpful and 2) not something we do for every prospect with whom we interact which together constitute the ultimate sign a rep has started to graduate from value-detracting salesperson to value-adding closer.

*

At Gartner I had a CTO prospect from one of my "must win" prospect organizations that I chased from my first day on the sales floor. He rejected me repeatedly, usually on the basis that while he found what Gartner provided to be of value to him personally, he'd never be able to get the necessary approvals to move forward.

I kept in contact with him nevertheless, usually be sending him industry research notes and webinars on topics I knew he was interested in from our conversations and from what he regular posted about on LinkedIn.

In a strange twist, he at one point told me that while it was unlikely he could partner *with Gartner* on a customer basis, he had interest in working *for* Gartner in a role that was highly coveted and one for which there were rarely openings. If he got the position in question I wouldn't be able to sell him anything, but I knew this was too great a chance to establish a strong sense of reciprocity to pass it up.

I offered to meet with him and discuss what I knew about the job and the skills he needed to show in order to land it, as well as refer him to HR. He didn't end up getting the position, but he was very grateful that I had gone so far out of my way to help him, seemingly when it wasn't in my own best interests to do so. I had moved myself in his subconscious from "Joe, Gartner sales rep," to "Joe, bro."

Later in the year I helped him again by getting him a complimentary pass to an event put on by our company. This was an event I knew he valued because he had paid to attend in previous years. I offered to get him there in exchange for doing a thorough reevaluation of our services with me on site, to which he gladly accepted.

At the event he and I met face-to-face for the first time. As he had in the past, he had gotten a lot out of the event and was thus in the best possible frame of mind I could ask for in terms of reevaluating our services. This time, instead of the prospect who had once told me he would never be able to get approval for a Gartner subscription, I had a prospect who was proactively offering creative ideas for how we might be able to accomplish just that.

When we got back to our respective offices we exchanged several emails over the course of the next month, which at various points involved 1) him almost signing, 2) him facing some internal difficulties in getting the agreement through procurement, and 3) a brief period where he went completely dark on me.

In July, roughly one month after the event, I sent him a 1-line text:

"This is ground control to Major Tom, can you hear me Major Tom?"

The next day I received a text back which read:

"This is Major Tom to ground control, sorry for being MIA..."

It turned out he couldn't sign for an agreement that would go into effect immediately, but he was willing to go ahead and commit dollars from next year's budget and sign an agreement that would start at the end of the fiscal year. He told me he had no reason to sign an agreement *now* that would not take effect for several months other than wanting to return the favor for the various ways I had gone above and beyond to help him personally during the preceding months.

*

Note that there are really two takeaways from the above anecdote. The first is that I had never done that particular combination of favors for another prospect, and he was cognizant of that. The Reciprocity Trigger loses its strength if that which is used to establish it is the same thing used by every rep at your company with every one of their prospects because your prospect will know whatever you're providing is par for the course.

The second alludes to something further discussed in the section on the 2nd Sale (below), and how the 2nd Sale is in part won before the 1st on account of which prospects you spend the majority of your time courting in the first place.

Simply put, I went to great lengths to establish the Reciprocity Trigger with this particular prospect because I knew he was the type of prospect that could ultimately build consensus to get Gartner's service passed within his organization.

Had I believed this wasn't the case, I wouldn't have spent so many hours trying to win him over only to fall flat when we got to this point.

As such, while the Reciprocity Trigger can be one of your greatest weapons in compelling your prospect forward, it tends to consume a lot of time and you must be guarded against establishing it within the minds of your prospects who don't have the ability to drive consensus around your company's product or service internally.

Even if you do have a prospect worthy of this treatment, it may not be possible to take such a strategic approach to establishing the Reciprocity Trigger, and I certainly did more for this prospect than was normal or even possible in most scenarios.

But that's exactly why it was so effective and why you must train yourself to be on the lookout for areas to add value to your prospect's life that are unique to that individual prospect such that they know damn well you're not doing the same thing for every other prospect with whom you come into contact.

Nonetheless, there *are* some tried and true ways to activate the Reciprocity Trigger described above, but again, the value you get out of doing something helpful for your prospect is going to increase dramatically the more tailored it is to that particular prospect and their organization:

1) A company resource – what this might be for you I can't say, as it depends entirely on the value proposition of your company, but the idea here is

you're able to provide them whatever it is that your company does in a trial or limited capacity such that you're able to help them without being of so much help there's now no longer any reason to buy from you. In other words, what you should do with "freebies" is help prospects start solving one or two problems to the extent that it hurts a little bit to think of you *out* of the picture from there on out.

2) Visiting your prospect on site – this is partly an appeal to ego. Very few of us don't enjoy being made to feel important. Most of your prospects will react positively to you dropping by to show them your commitment to them. It gets their subconscious to whisper, "she took all that time to come out here to meet with you face to face, you should at least take a meeting with her."

3) An oft-overlooked but potent means of establishing the Reciprocity Trigger is looking out not only for your prospect, but also the members of their 360 – the people that report to them, their peers, and their superiors.

   The Digital Era is one in which we are uber aware and concerned about what others think of us, an exacerbation of the social tiers of Maslow's Pyramid due in part to how connected we are to one another all the time. Thus, the value here is making your prospect look good by doing something that is of value to members of their team (and letting your prospect know you've done that, of course). This has the added benefit of warming up other stakeholders involved in the decision-making process later on in the sales cycle.

   Whatever you do for your prospect, do not forget to make your efforts compellingly relevant to what's most important to them. Also, take care not to conflate reciprocity with periodically just throwing freebies at your prospect. If not uniquely tailored to their needs, giving away time and resources for nothing in return only subjugates you to the prospect and erodes any semblance of the Authority Trigger you've built in their subconscious to this point.

7. Mental Trigger 5 - Trust & Liking

"Few people would be surprised to learn that, as a rule, we prefer to say yes to the requests of someone we know and like." – Robert B. Cialdini

In the same vein as the above quote, I doubt many salespeople would be surprised to learn that they are more likely to close a deal if their prospect(s) like them.

Does this mean that your prospect is going to sign a deal with you solely because you're boys? Definitely not. The payoff of the Trust & Liking trigger shouldn't be undervalued, however, as it has the power to win those deals at the margins.

To see why this is true, consider everything your prospects have going on in their day to day lives, both professionally and personally.

If your prospect is like most prospects, they are C-Level executives or otherwise with significant responsibilities within their organizations. There are going to be a myriad of things that could get in the way of them signing your service agreement or product order during the time period in which you need it signed, even if that's entirely their intention.

Simply put, the more your prospect likes you, the more likely it is that they find a way to push past all the distractions and get the agreement signed in the 11th hour regardless. That's partly the Reciprocity Trigger at work too, of course, but it's also because we want the people we like to like us in return... and there's no better way to get a sales rep to like you than by sending them a signed agreement.

Trust & Liking is a difficult mental trigger for the average sales rep to establish because most prospects (& people) aren't predisposed to like salespeople. If you think of the stereotypical image of the "salesman," it isn't great. It's the used car salesman in a cheap tie that's tied too short, a little too eager to greet us when we come onto the lot. It's the "fast-talking" salesman that's out to get us to sign on the dotted line regardless of whether it's in our best interests.

There was undoubtedly more truth to these negative associations in the past, when sales reps had the power of information asymmetry on their side.

In the pre-Digital Era, before the advent and exponential increase in the consumption of the internet, buyers were less able to educate themselves on just how much they should be paying for that used car, or whether it really was the one best suited to their needs.

In these situations, dishonest sales reps were able to say a lot without a ton of repercussion because consumers didn't have a way to fact check their claims before signing.

Today these associations have less of a basis in reality, particularly in B2B sales where sales reps are usually dealing with savvy prospects with years of corporate buying experience which includes an MBA in sniffing out bullshit. Even reps who would otherwise lack any sense of morality in their sales practices know they can't trick a prospect into signing an agreement through smoke and mirrors.

The negative mental association prospects have of sales reps is still there, however, and its staying power is due to the conditioning from society's appetite for exaggerating stereotypes. *Glengarry Glen Ross* & *The Wolf of Wall Street* are two popular examples. The characters in these movies reinforce the negative associations most people have with salespeople and make us hesitant to engage with them.

(As an aside, the general dislike & distrust of the sales rep is in-and-of-itself a complete argument against relying upon discovery questions as your principal sales strategy. I mean, we're seriously going to rely on soliciting information from people who are predisposed to distrust us as our primary means of generating interest and advancing a deal forward? Ok.)

It makes sense, then, that to establish the Trust & Liking Trigger within our prospect's subconscious, we must first disassociate ourselves from the pre-established negative perception our prospect has of us already.

There's good news here. By working to establish the Mental Triggers we've discussed thus far, you've already begun to break that association. This is why Trust & Liking is the last of the Mental Triggers to be established in the mind of your prospect; it is in part the effect of all the other Mental Triggers combined.

Nevertheless, it's one thing to break the preconditioned negative association your prospect has of you, and another altogether to get them to genuinely *like* you. Breaking the negative association of "sales rep" really just gets us to a place of neutrality, not favoritism. How do we take it that additional step?

First, let's consider some of the things that make us more inclined to like certain people in general:

1. Physical Appearance – study after study has shown that we are predisposed to like people that are well put together because we subconsciously ascribe positive character traits like honesty, intelligence, and talent to those people.

    While there is of course a limit to what we can do about our physical appearance, what's important to consider is that you at least give yourself a chance for it to influence your prospect in the right way. Dress like a pro and keep your hygiene immaculate.

    If you're in inside sales, which I suspect a lot of you are, physical appearance may be less of a factor. But for the love of God, make sure you have a LinkedIn picture that isn't you and the boys getting weird in the back of frat row.

    Humans make snap judgements of one another based on appearance alone, so why would you put yourself behind the 8-ball before you even get a chance to meet with your prospect by looking you lack the common sense in even choosing a picture to represent you professionally?

2. Similarity – it comes as no surprise that we gravitate towards people that are similar to us, or possess traits we would also like to possess.

    At first glance this doesn't do us much good – the average sales rep has little in common with his prospect, professionally or personally. For one, the average sales rep tends to be younger, without children, and has markedly different interests than the C-Level executive with 30 years' experience, three failed marriages, and a $10M net worth.

When there isn't much of substance with which we can connect to our prospects, the tendency of most reps is to engage in the sort of superficial rapport building that you'll still find subtlety recommended in many a common sales rag.

The problem with trying to make yourself more like your prospect by bringing up your shared love for UNC Basketball during every meeting, however, is that it's so far removed from the context of what brought the two of you together in the first place that it has a negative effect on the other mental triggers.

Similarly, if you find yourself with a prospect who is willing to spend an undue amount of time over this type of "rapport building," you likely haven't gone after the type of prospect who can get anything done during the 2nd Sale (see below). If you had, they wouldn't have the time to spend pandering to your cheesy ass ☺.

When possible, keep rapport building tactics focused around professional similarities first, and use personal similarities only sparingly in an attempt to get your prospect to develop a personal affinity towards you.

3. Transparency

The trigger is named *Trust* & Liking for a reason, and when all of our good looks and similar areas of interest fail us in getting our prospect to feel the warm and fuzzies every time she thinks of us, transparency is what helps us get over the hump.

Simply put, transparency is what breeds trust, and we like people we can trust. A lot, in fact.

During my sales career I've found I've usually had nothing to lose by opening the kimono. Initially it was something I relied upon because it made me more comfortable early on in my sales career when I didn't have as much subject matter expertise as I'd like to be compellingly relevant during my meetings with prospects.

It was simply easier for me to admit where I lacked expertise in a particular area relative to my prospect than to try to bullshit, and so long as I continued to focus on making the best use of their time, my prospects generally responded positively to helping me fill in the gaps.

With experience I began to look for opportunities to be more strategically transparent with my prospects by revealing information they might not expect me to reveal.

Below is an example of this strategic type of transparency, used in this instance during a situation I shouldn't have put myself in to begin with:

After I had moved up to Gartner's Large Enterprise division, I was deep in a sales cycle with the CIO of a university who had given me a ballpark budget to work around when making service recommendations.

It just so happened that at this particular point in time senior leadership was really pushing a service that was outside his price range, and I had a unique set of factors pressuring me into proposing a solution that was far out of bounds from what he had shared with me.

When I presented him with a service proposal which was almost double his stated budget, there was an audible sigh on the other end of the phone, followed by something to the effect of:

"So, when you put this thing together, did you just completely disregard that we've discussed my budget a couple of times now already?"

Damn, Daniel.

I rather meekly attempted to justify a service recommendation I knew I shouldn't have proposed in the first place before the conversation ended with me eating crow and convincing him to regroup with me the next day so I could put something in front of him more aligned with his budget.

Prior to hanging up, he told me how set he had been on partnering with Gartner during to our previous conversations, but he didn't want to partner with any firm that was only looking to take him for a ride.

It was a personally poignant indictment and an implicit statement telling me I had completely destroyed any Trust & Liking I had previously established.

With it in mind that I had to rectify the damage I had done, I decided what would be best moving forward was for me to be radically transparent with my prospect.

And so, when pitching him on the new service recommendation, I pulled up the company intranet and internal pricing database, which included the bare minimums for which reps were able to sell the different services we provided to customers. In doing so, my prospect was able to see beyond a doubt that what I was proposing was based exclusively on his needs and not any ulterior motives. This strategy had the added benefit of eliminating the need to have any additional meeting to negotiate over price, and I was promptly rewarded for my transparency with a signed contract the next day.

A final note on the Trust & Liking trigger. Aside from liking people that are similar to us and transparent in how they deal with us, we also find value in people that are happy. That are confident. That are excited to be doing what they're doing. I'm not sure writing additional sections on these character traits would be a meaningful use of your time, but always bear in mind that no matter what's going on in your world externally, you owe it to yourself and your prospect to bring a certain amount of juice to your meetings.

8. The 2nd Sale

You have won the 1st Sale after firmly establishing all five of the above Mental Triggers within the subconscious of your prospect and they have become positively inclined towards getting something done with you over all the other, value-detracting sales reps they could work with to solve the challenges which have brought the two of you together instead.

The spoils for your efforts are that the two of you are now working from the same side of the table. You are two closers, and that which is sitting across from you now is any number of key stakeholders within your prospect's organization your prospect must convince of the value your company's product or service will bring to the table.

Enabling them to do this successfully is what constitutes the 2nd Sale.

It is during the 2nd Sale where discovery questions actually have the most value. Unlike your initial meeting when your prospect has yet to see any real value in exchange for the sales ammo you're requesting they provide you, your prospect is now just as incentivized in answering your questions as you are in asking them.

Moreover, you're now in a position to ask the type of questions which have the power to greatly increase a deal's velocity to closure; the type of questions which would make your prospect bristle had you not already won the 1st Sale. Questions like, "who in your organization is most likely to shoot this thing down, and what are we going to do about it?"

On the whole, any question you have your prospect answer during the 2nd Sale should be geared towards putting him or her in the best possible position to convince other stakeholders within their organization of the value of your company's product or service is going to bring to the table.

"Wait a minute," you say, "I don't want to put my deal in the hands of someone who doesn't know how to sell. Shouldn't I just get in front of all those other stakeholders myself?"

Getting multiple stakeholders involved early in your sales cycle could be a good thing. It could also be a terrible thing, and that's because you haven't had the opportunity to complete the 1st Sale with each of these people the way you have with your individual prospect.

As such, you put yourself at tremendous risk of encountering a stakeholder negatively predisposed towards your company's product or service without an opportunity to change their disposition, spoiling the party for the rest of the group.

Even if that's not the case with the particular prospect organization with which we're presently dealing, you're very rarely going to be able to meet with *everyone* that matters during *every* meeting you orchestrate and conduct.

Moreover, with any new stakeholders attending a meeting for the first time, your primary focus with these individuals includes completing (another) 1st Sale with each in addition to completing the 2nd.

When you aggregate all the additional hours it requires to do this with every stakeholder at your prospect organization, the "I'll close them all myself" mentality starts to make very little sense as an MO.

Presuming you can orchestrate one big meeting with everyone at the end of a sales cycle to close the 2nd Sale is also misguided. None of your prospect's colleagues are going to become convinced to spend thousands of dollars on your company's product or service after a single meeting. The truth is that if you've gotten to this point, it is because your prospect has been successful working these individuals in the background already.

Indeed, it is far more useful to treat the 2nd Sale as what's accomplished by your prospect *only* when you're not around to sell for them. It helps to distinguish things this way in order to remember that part of your job is influencing the chances of a deal's success when you're not in the picture to persuade key stakeholders yourself.

What have you done to influence the internal dynamics in which you're not going to be privy? What have you done to equip your prospect, now champion, for success?

As mentioned previously, this is where discovery questions are most effective, as you're able to zero in on just that information needed from your prospect to directly influence your chances of helping them when you're not in the immediate picture.

Bearing in mind that you should always give context to the questions you're asking so as not to insult your prospect's intelligence, the sorts of questions you should ask at this stage include:

1) How are you going to frame the value of our service to other members of the organization?

   What you're essentially doing with this question is hearing how your prospect plans to pitch your product or service internally. Most of your prospects aren't going to be natural closers, and this is your one opportunity to critique and correct where needed.

   What you're primarily looking for is that your prospect isn't encapsulating the value of what your company provides in a completely self-serving capacity. For example if you're selling a leaning management system (LMS) to a hospital administrator which enables all of his nurses and staff to be able to complete their state and federally mandated training requirements more efficiently online, you want him translating these benefits into metrics that matter to the organization's financial health as a whole – metrics pertaining to risk, growth & cost.

   What you *don't* want is your prospect telling the Board or executive management "this is going to make my job a lot easier by freeing up more of my time to attend to other matters."

   That might be exactly how he encapsulates the value of what you provide by default, but the Board very likely does not give a single fuck how many hours your administrator stands to save by procuring your company's LMS. You can be certain, however, that the Board cares about the ongoing financial viability of the hospital. And, while it might seem obvious to your prospect that the time he and his staff save on training will result in a reduction in the training expenses which affects the entire hospital, other stakeholders cannot be relied upon to make this leap automatically.

2. Are there any stakeholders that might try to shoot us down? Why?

The authors of *The Challenger Customer* found that once a decision-making group reaches 5 or more individuals, the likelihood of that group coming to a consensus to sign an agreement with a vendor drops drastically in favor of sticking with the status quo. This is because each stakeholder in the decision-making group is going to have a different role and set of responsibilities that cause them to look for different benefits in a vendor product or service.

For example, in order to keep expenses manageable, a CFO is responsible for earmarking funds only for new investments with clearly demonstrable ROI, whereas a Chief Revenue Officer is metriced primarily on how much growth she can bring to the organization quarter over quarter.

The incentives of these two people differ drastically, which when extrapolated to the interests of multiple stakeholders means multiple combinations of incentives potentially at odds with one another. As such, consensus around your product or service can become more and more unlikely as the decision-making group increases in number.

You want your prospect to understand these risks so they don't end up organizing an unduly large decision-making council for your product or service when the two of you might otherwise determine that the only people that really need to sign off on the deal are two other stakeholders with incentives similar to your prospect's.

If the decision-making group is going to be relatively large, you'll have wanted to at least have brought this to light so that the two of you can strategize on how to best overcome any naysaying jabronis that might otherwise try to shoot the deal down.

3. What else can I provide you to maximize our chances for success?

No matter what you've done during the 1st Sale, it's sure to have included a mix of presentations, executive summaries, and business cases.

It is unlikely that a piece of collateral is going to decide a deal one way or the other, but we can't discount the idea that there might be something we could provide our prospect that would make the situation a lot easier on them internally, and something for which they're neglecting to ask us because they simply don't realize they can.

What sort of materials has your prospect found to encapsulate the value of what you're providing to the prospect's organization best? Do they need something else? An ROI calculator? A cost-benefit analysis? What? Don't rely on them telling you what this might be without you prompting them.

9. The 2nd Sale is Won Before the 1st

The reality that it is your prospect that will ultimately be the one to complete the 2nd Sale has important implications that are ignored by many sales organizations.

While most new reps are instructed to tier their prospect organizations – "must win," "tier 1", "tier 2," etc. – less frequently are they instructed to tier their individual prospects within these prospect organizations. I'm not necessarily recommending that's something you do, either, and you'll have to make a judgment call on whether it's worth the time to do something like this for all your prospect organizations.

At the very least, however, you should have a list of "must win" prospects at "must win" prospect organizations. These are the individual prospects you feel have the most ability and propensity to get the 2nd Sale finalized internally. If you think about it, what you're trying to do is find the prospects which are themselves closers...at those organizations which have the most propensity to be closed.

This is extremely important. During the course of the year you're going to have the opportunity to work with a variety of prospects with varying degrees of desire and ability to get shit done.

The time you spend on the prospect who kicks tires or drags their feet getting things accomplished internally is the time you could have spent finding the rising star hired recently at one of your prospect organizations specifically to play the role of corporate change agent (as gleaned from the press release upon their hiring, for example). These are the prospects with whom you should strive to spend your time, as they are best suited to drive consensus among stakeholders and thus most capable of completing the 2nd Sale.

This person's role in you ultimately closing the deal cannot be understated. Remember that even if you get in front of your prospect's key stakeholders/executive management team on multiple occasions, very rarely are they going to sign with you present because they're going to want to finalize agreement among themselves internally first.

And that's exactly when the personality conflicts & office politics you're not seeing begin to rear their ugly heads, and there are key stakeholders out of the office unexpectedly, or a flakey stakeholder starts waffling on their support for your product or service after a couple of days go by.

Do you really have control over all of these things? Are you going to go on-site to your prospect's organization and get a detailed report of who's taking time off and when so you can put the agreement in front of the whole group to get it completed in one fell swoop? No, of course you're not, and this is why picking the correct prospects in which you prioritize your time and efforts is paramount to your success.

While "discovery first" sales methodologies might offer the most misguided sales advice for closers in the Digital Era, the consequences of choosing which prospects we go after in the first place might be some of the least discussed. For too often do reps allocate their time to prospects as if there aren't wild differences among them in terms of ability of getting anything accomplished internally.

To most sales methodologies, a prospect is a prospect is a prospect, and while these books are replete with example after example of the "right" questions to ask prospects during different situations, very few acknowledge that it takes the right prospects for the answers to these questions to have any real value in the first place.

The Challenger Customer is the only book out there I've seen which gives this vital component of closing its due. It does a great job of going into extensive detail about which traits identify prospects as having the propensity to get a deal accomplished internally, which importantly includes the ability to drive consensus towards something new and away from the status quo.

10. The 1ˢᵗ & 2ⁿᵈ Sale, Together

1. Buying preferences of the Digital Era have created a
    B2C economy where time-value has become a chief
    competitive differentiator among businesses (e.g.
    Amazon and other algorithmically-driven
    organizations).

    The B2B environment is not immune to the effects of
    this shift, and prospects will subconsciously begin to
    expect more value from the B2B buying experiences
    which currently resemble anything but the buying
    experiences they have become accustomed to having
    in their day to day lives.

2. Consultative, discovery-oriented sales methodologies
    are anathema to this socio-economic shift when relied
    on exclusively to move a deal forward. That's because
    instead of *providing* prospects with more value for
    their time, these methodologies train reps to *solicit*
    value from them instead. This results in the prospect
    feeling as though meeting with the sales rep is poor
    use of their most coveted need... their time.

3. While B2B buying experiences cannot mimic the algorithmically driven experiences of the B2C arena, it is vital that the closer takes it upon herself to bridge the gap between current B2C and B2B buying experiences by personally delivering more value in each and every interaction with her prospects.

   In doing so, her prospects will become psychologically inclined to want to work with the closer and her company over reps from other companies still focused on soliciting value rather than providing it.

4. Prospects in B2B sales feel they are receiving value form the closer when the closer has activated and strengthened a series of five Mental Triggers within the prospect's subconscious which tells the prospect that the closer is making excellent use of their time.

   These triggers are "felt" by the prospect, not consciously contemplated. If they were, they would look something like this:

   a. Compelling Relevance – "I am working with a rep who has approached me about being able to solve a challenge which is of compelling relevance to my interests. They have displayed a uniquely deep understanding of this challenge, much more so than other sales reps."

   b. Authority – "I am working with a rep whose opinion I respect, and I find myself tending to believe whatever comes out of their mouth based on how they communicate it."

   c. Consistency – I am working with a rep that brings value to each and every interaction I have with them. Because they are able to do this so consistently, I'm sure the product or service they represent can too. I would not hesitate to put them in front of my CEO & CFO because they've never shown a propensity to drop the ball.

   d. Reciprocity – "I am working with a rep who has done some pretty unique things to help me already, and I'm not even a customer yet!"

   e. Trust & Liking – I am working with a rep I genuinely like, and who I know has never tried to hoodwink me into something that wasn't in my best interests.

5. After having begun to establish these Mental Triggers in the mind of the prospect, discovery questions now have more value to both prospect and closer, as the prospect is now psychologically inclined to want to get a deal accomplished and thus more likely to provide answers that actually move the deal forward.

6. The 2nd Sale represents the point in time during a sales cycle when the prospect has begun to play from the same side of the table as the closer, and they have become united in the common goal of enabling the prospect to become a customer.

   It also represents the point in time when the closer's role becomes preparing the prospect for the obstacles they will face in getting the internal agreement necessary to move forward with the closer, and equipping them accordingly.

7. Due to the rise of the consensus sale, your prospect's ability to breed agreement among a group of stakeholders with disparate incentives is becoming more and more critical to whether the closer is ultimately successful in obtaining a signature. As

such, the 2nd Sale is partly won before the 1st Sale on the basis of the closer selecting the right prospects to pursue in the first place.

"It always seems impossible until it is done." – Nelson Mandela

Part II: The Mental Manual

1. Sales as a Game of Chess

"These young guys are playing checkers. I'm out there playing chess." – Kobe Bryant

Checkers is a game of limited, uniform moves, which is how a lot of sales reps treat their profession: the daily carrying out of a uniform, finite set of moves that mirror those which other reps on the sales floor are making.

A closer plays chess. Chess is a game that necessitates a constant awareness of the many moves a player *could* make and opting for the one that has the greatest chance of success given the unique circumstances at that point in time. A closer is also aware of the moves everyone else is making but does not presume they are correct. In fact, because most reps experience mediocre results, the closer presumes the moves that most reps are making to be wrong.

Example 1: Prospecting Emails

Anybody in sales will tell you how important prospecting is in creating a steady stream of new deals in play. Yet prospecting is universally abhorred, in part because the amount of effort it can take to get meetings with people who have previously shown no interest in us can feel immense, particularly when we can't get so much as a reply from them.

Reps have a tendency to think that if a prospect hasn't replied to their email, then they aren't interested in taking a meeting. If this is you, you're making the assumption that your prospect has even noticed your email in the first place.

I'd wager that most prospect emails are deleted without a prospect having ever seen their contents. It's especially likely considering that most reps send prospecting emails at the times when reps from every other company trying to get ahold of their prospect are also sending them emails, people within their own company are sending them emails, and they're least receptive to being interrupted.

What if instead of sending prospect emails at the same times as everyone else competing for our prospect's attention we sent them at more unorthodox hours when we have to compete with less noise. What if we sent our prospects emails on the weekends, for example?

There are advantages to this line of thinking:

First, you immediately begin to show your prospect's subconscious you're not the same kind of average, value-detracting sales rep they run into so often. If you don't get a reply straight away, they're at least more likely to remember who you are during your next attempt, and you have thus begun to pull yourself out of the anonymity that cloaks the vast majority of sales prospecting efforts due to the sheer volume/annoyance levels created by the confluence of spammy emails all received by your prospect during the same timeframe each day.

Second, because you're contacting your prospect when their inbox isn't already being flooded by everyone else, the chances your prospect actually reads the body of your email rather than just skimming the subject line and deleting it improve quite a bit.

A favorite email that I'd send prospects on a Sunday, particularly if I hadn't gotten any momentum going during the week with them would go something like this:

"John – attempting to break through the noise here, as I'm sure you're inundated with emails during the week. I've reattached the offer I mentioned in my last email. We would only need 15 minutes to determine if there's a basis for us to continue conversations. Are you available Tuesday at 4pm for 15 minutes?

I've thought through every line of this email. First, I tell the prospect straight away about the sort of rep I am; one that's strategic in breaking through the noise that would otherwise drown out my email along with all the rest. I have innocuously begun establishing the Authority Trigger in my prospect's subconscious in this subliminal show of competence.

Second, I make it easy for them to see the offer to which I've alluded. By putting it in an attachment I make good use of their time by not making them have to search back through their inbox to find the original email I'm referencing (as if that has any chance of happening) to view the offer.

By putting the offer in an attachment, we lessen the chance of our prospect losing interest in an overly wordy body of the email before they get to the actual offer itself.

We've structured the body of the email to be so short and to the point that the prospect can read the whole thing just by glancing at it. And when they open the attachment, they'll find an offer similarly short and sweet that can be read and digested in one fell swoop of the eyeballs.

Next, we recommend one specific time for a meeting. It isn't Monday, a day in which most prospects don't want to schedule *anything* because they're too busy catching up on the work that's piled up from the week before. It isn't Wednesday, because we already have two meetings scheduled that day for which we'll need time to prepare. No, it's Tuesday, because out of all our options Tuesday gives us the best chance to both land the meeting and give it the proper amount of attention it deserves. 4pm is chosen because we believe it maximizes our chances of our prospect being done with his internal meetings by that point in the day.

Further along, I've only asked my prospect for 15 minutes. Whereas most reps are asking my prospect for 30 minutes, or even an hour for the stereotypical, value-detracting discovery meeting. I'm betting on myself that I can begin establishing the Mental Triggers that constitute the 1st Sale thoroughly enough in the first 15 minutes that my prospect will at that point commit to another, more substantive meeting.

Finally, I allude to the idea that I'm not sure if there's going to be a basis for us to continue a conversation at the end of our meeting. This is a bit of strategically-placed transparency, as it may make the prospect feel more comfortable taking a meeting with a rep that is up front in conceding the meeting not go anywhere (even if we're sure it will).

That's a lot of thought that's gone into an email that is technically only two sentences long, but wouldn't you agree that I've increased my odds of scoring a meeting with John over the reps that are waiting until Monday morning when he's already in the throes of work, in a foul mood, and mass-deleting sales emails with righteous prejudice?

How might we continue playing chess from this point?

Let's say John doesn't reply to us right away (he probably won't). Should I send a follow up email the next day? A closer might think it over and come to the conclusion that the prospect is likely to interpret this as "I'm desperate to get a response from you" and decide to circle back on Tuesday instead:

John – circling back here in case this got lost in the shuffle. How's Thursday at 11am? Note that I'm also willing to meet outside of normal business hours if that's more convenient for you (Thursday at 6pm?).

Again, there's a lot of strategic intent here that's packed into a very short email.

First, we strike a tone that we're completely unphased to this point that John has blown us off. In conveying the assumption that John should want to meet with us, we again suggest a meeting time, but this time we insert a strategic twist: we offer to meet with John outside of normal working hours.

By offering to go the extra mile and meet before or after business hours, we again tickle the Authority Trigger in John's subconscious. We're signaling, "I take my job seriously and I'll gladly work more hours than normal if that's' what it takes. I'm not running out of the office as soon as the clock strikes 5pm like the kiddos with whom you're used to dealing."

I've also started to put my finger on the Reciprocity Trigger. If I'm willing to go above and beyond for a meeting with you, you'll at least feel more inclined to offer up a response, whether it be acceptance or to offer an excuse for why the proposed time doesn't work.

Finally, we're banking that we're establishing a bit of the Trust & Liking Trigger as well. Remember that we like people that are similar to us, and here we're signaling to the prospect that like them, we are hard workers.

People that have worked hard to achieve the success they've had typically like young people that demonstrate these traits as well. Chances are that applies to your prospect presuming you're going after the senior decisionmakers of an organization.

Example 2: Cold Calls

Just like sending emails to prospects when everyone else is doing the same thing, it doesn't make sense to call prospects during times when we're faced with another wave of competition doing just that, either.

Personally, I found that if I made calls to my prospects before or after work (say 7:15am -8am and 5:30pm to 6:30pm), I had a much higher success rate getting through to my prospect and setting a meeting.

By limiting when we call our prospects to times when most people are not, we increase the probability of reaching our prospect in part because the chances they are already busy speaking or responding to someone else are almost none existent.

Additionally, because our prospects are likely to have receptionists or assistants working 8-5, we have limited our prospecting times to when we are least likely to get blocked by a gatekeeper. Gatekeepers, after all, are trained to not let most people through to their boss.

While many of our prospects will be used to arriving early and staying late, it's doubtful they expect their receptionists/assistants to work the same hours. So, why not start making your calls when you face less competition both from your peers *drowning you out* as well as from gatekeepers *shutting you out?*

Example 3: Prospect Voicemails

If you've been at this for a little while, chances are you've left hundreds of voicemails for your prospects, with very, very (very) [like infinitesimally] few being returned. And, if you're like most reps, you tend to leave your voicemails the same way each time:

"Hey Jim, it's Joe with Gartner. I was just giving you a ring to..."

"Hi Sharon, it's Joe from Gartner. I was calling you to..."

"Hi Dan, it's Joe..."

Playing chess here might involve a closer examining the way he's been leaving voicemails and determining that the cadence of his voicemails has become too familiar to the prospect.

He sees this is a problem because he's left this prospect voicemails in the past and they have failed to produce any action on the prospect's part, so leaving this prospect similar voicemails now leaves a very good chance of them just deleting his voicemails as soon as they recognize the cadence which gives him away:

Voicemail 1) "Hi Jim, it's Joe from Gartner. I was calling to invite you to Gartner's Security Summit. It's..." *Jim Deletes*

Voicemail 2) Hi Jim, it's Joe from Gartn..." *Jim Deletes*

Voicemail 3) "Hi Jim, it's J..." *Jim Deletes*

Voicemail 4) Deleted upon recognition of number

Voicemail 5) Deleted upon recognition of number

You can see in these examples that I'm playing checkers, and so too do I play my own checkers-playing ass. Although it might feel productive to leave prospect voicemails, they're a total waste of time if your prospects are not listening to them.

How might I play chess here instead? Knowing that my prospect is likely to start deleting my voicemails immediately if they recognize my cadence, I take a different approach:

Voicemail 1) "Hi Jim, it's Joe with Gartner, I was giving you a ring to invite you to the Gartner Security Summit. If..." *Jim Deletes*

Voicemail 2) I forgot to mention yesterday, your invitation includes the ability to bring your CISO with you on a complimentary basis as well. Give me a ring back when you get this. Joe Duval with Gartner 919-963-1234

Voicemail 3) Jim, it's Joe shooting you an email here momentarily because we only have 6 days left for me to secure you that complimentary pass to the event. These tickets are normally $3,500. Check your inbox.

These voicemails are superior because, if I miss on the first voicemail (as indicated in the example), I don't give my prospect an opportunity to recognize it's me again on the second.

By switching up the cadence of my voicemails, the ebb and flow if you will, I don't give Jim the opportunity to go into insta-delete mode.

Put yourself in Jim's shoes and take a look at voicemail #2. By starting the voicemail without any introduction, wouldn't your initial reaction be a slightly confused *yet intrigued* "what the fuck?"

You might think someone is leaving you a voicemail by accident. In any case, aren't you now listening to this bizarre voicemail that has begun in medias res?

Notice it isn't until the end that I leave my contact information in the form of a sign off. At that point Jim has very likely listened to the whole message increasing my odds dramatically that he'll hear the important part about the complimentary pass to the Security Summit. Contrast this with the earlier examples; we've now created a situation where Jim hears an offer he finds valuable whereas before he didn't hear it at all.

The 3rd voicemail also holds Jim's attention. As he's listening, he's thinking "wait, who is this sending me an email? Do I have a relationship with this person? The pass he wants to give me is worth how much?"

And, because chess connotes a game in which we're always thinking a few moves ahead, we've primed him to expect an email that will contain details of the offer with which we've now been successful piquing his interest.

Example 4: Email Trackers

The way most reps use email trackers is to lean over to our buddy sitting beside us and whispering excitedly, "Randy just opened that email I sent him about the end of year offer," followed by a short team prayer where you and your comrades pray to the deal gods for a commission-positive response.

Consider how much more value we'd get if, instead of getting all worked up from knowing that our prospect has in that moment recognized our existence, we picked up the phone and called them right then and there? When throughout the course of the day could we ever be so sure our prospect is currently thinking of us *and* by their phone?

Yet in this situation most reps do exactly as I first described and wait for a response that never comes. What if that response never came because your prospect had a couple of questions that she could have asked you if she had you on the line?

Another way we could use email trackers more effectively is to use them as a measuring stick to gauge our prospects' interest in us. Both HubSpot and Yesware (to my knowledge, two of the more prominent email trackers on the market) will show you not only that a prospects has clicked an email, but how many times they've opened it, whether they've forwarded it to other stakeholders, whether they've also looked at any attachments you've included, etc.

If a prospect clicks on an email multiple times, has forwarded it to additional contacts, or has opened your attachments, you probably have a prospect who has seen a potential reason for engaging with you. When they are forwarding your attachments to others in the organization for example, what do you think that looks like?

Probably a lot of emails to the effect of "A Gartner rep just sent this to me. They might be able to help with our CRM overhaul, should we set up some time with him?"

Playing chess in this capacity gives you a structured way to turn up the heat on prospects based on whose mind you're already on.

Hey, you're never going to have a better chance of setting a meeting with a prospect than when they're already inclined to say "yes." If you make a habit of going through your email opens at the end of the day, perhaps you could turn a lot of would-be cold outreach attempts into warm ones by targeting those prospects you know are already thinking about you.

Example 5: LinkedIn

LinkedIn is another example where the vast majority of reps play checkers. It's an example that's particularly adverse to their interests, too, because in doing so they tell their entire business network in one fell swoop what kind of rep they are.

Most reps use LinkedIn as an advertising platform for meetings, generally by sharing content they didn't author or collateral promoting how sweet their company is. They tend to conclude these posts with something to the effect of "message me if you're interested in seeing how we can help bolster your cyber security program against ransomware attacks!"

Remember that the Digital Era means as closers we must signal to our prospects that we are the type of people with whom interacting would be good, regardless of the products and services we represent. This signals the opposite. This signals "contact me if you want to be sold on something."

You might see that in using LinkedIn like this what we end up doing is not only posting something that's going to generate zero responses, but also erode our ability to establish the Mental Triggers we've discussed at length...before you've even had the opportunity to directly speak to your prospect!

For example, say you're a Chief Information Officer who has just accepted my invitation to connect. My invitation to connect reads:

"Hi Amy, I thought connecting with you would be a good way for us to expand our professional networks."

Even though I've told Amy the basis for our connection was net-working, she quickly sees that what I really use LinkedIn for is to try and get more sales meetings.

Once she sees this, do you think she's going to be more or less likely to meet with me than she would have been had I never connected with her in the first place? Is she more or less inclined to trust me?

If I do somehow end up getting a meeting with her, she'll go into that meeting with her subconscious on high alert that I'm probably not going to be the type of person with whom she'll want to spend a lot of time. Not a great place to start, since it's a lot harder to establish the Mental Triggers in our prospect's subconscious once it has begun viewing us in a negative light.

How might we leverage LinkedIn if we were playing chess instead?

One idea is instead of posting content amounting to thinly veiled advertising, we could use LinkedIn to publish our own content on topics of compelling relevance to our prospects.

This has the opposite effect of using LinkedIn as an advertising platform, as we're now starting to establish the Mental Triggers in the minds of our prospects instead of eroding them. For example, we signal both Compelling Relevance & Authority in our ability to contribute our proprietary thoughts to a conversation in which your prospect actively participates.

And, if you recall from our analysis of the Trust & Liking trigger, we increase our likeability by showing prospects we are more like them and less like the typical sales robot they have had plenty of misfortune meeting in the past. In this example, you've used LinkedIn to warm up your prospects before you even try to set a meeting with them.

Using LinkedIn in this capacity yields to us another benefit. Recall that for your prospect to want to meet with you over multiple meetings, you must not only make sure to keep all interactions relevant to their interests, but compellingly so.

As discussed, it's very difficult to be compellingly relevant in the mind of our prospects if we don't have a deep, empathetic understanding of their world. Earlier in the book I discussed a learning technique for getting to that point of expertise more quickly, but another way to actively learn about your prospect's world is to force ourselves to share our own thoughts on the topic at hand. Like the imagery technique, it's a form of *active* learning, which increases our chances of being able to recall the relevant information when it would be beneficial during a meeting with a prospect.

Think about it, young rainmaker, with which rep is your prospect more likely to meet? The one who has already shown their ability to understand the world in which that prospect inhabits, or the sales parrot who "would love to take 30 minutes of your time to better understand your priorities for the year"? Which rep has signaled value for the prospect, and which is trying to solicit it?

One last note on LinkedIn. If you pay for LinkedIn Sales Navigator, you have the ability to send prospects messages with attachments before those prospects are even connected with you. A lot of reps use this feature to send prospects messages asking for meetings. If this you, STOP it with your checkers-playing ass! The only thing you're doing is showing your prospects straight away that they don't want to meet with you.

A more strategic way to use this feature would be to send collateral of genuine value to your prospect without asking for anything in return in that particular message:

"Hi Amy, saw this article on HBR and thought of something you had posted recently. Maybe it will be useful to you?"

I've left the door open for Amy to respond, but even if she doesn't immediately I've signaled the right things to her. And over the course of the year by continuing to do so while remaining consistent in reaching out to her frequently, we're damn sure going to get a meeting eventually.

*

Sales is a glorious game of chess for the young closer who thinks through their moves this way, and while the above illustrations are meant to be useful examples, the important takeaway here is that you develop a habitual awareness of how you currently do things so you can make continuous, iterative improvements to each holistic element of your sales process.

Where are you currently playing checkers simply because you've failed to consider whether there are superior ways to carry out that particular part of your sales process?

My hunch is you will be surprised by how little you've thought through a lot of what you're currently doing. I was. Once this initial disappointment wears off, however, you will be sold on the value of making awareness habitual when your meetings pick up and the paychecks get heavier.

2. Presence Produces the Presents

"Real generosity toward the future lies in giving all to the present." – Albert Camus

A Buddha-like ability to stay present might not be the first characteristic that springs to mind when you think "closer," but it is in many ways the mental aspect of an elite closer that allows everything else to flourish in the first place.

Let's go back to setting meetings via cold call for a moment. There are very few people that experience an innate joy from picking up the phone and calling someone who is not expecting to hear from them, nor pleased when they realize they've picked up the phone for a sales call.

But, when we really break it down, where does the negative reaction you experience from the words "cold call" come into play?

Is it a feeling that's created by what's going on in this present moment, or is it because you're remembering how a prospect took your head off last week and imagining it happening again?

It is important that we orient ourselves towards presence so that we don't let what *may* happen prevent us from taking any action at all. Fixating on past results and believing future outcomes will mirror them can trap us into overthinking just about everything we do.

In a state of presence, however, we are able to see the task at hand just for what it is: an independent event the result of which is unaffected by any like-event of the past. It is in this mind state that we are able to execute much more efficiently.

I say "orient ourselves towards presence" instead of "stay present" because the latter would be an impossible task to ask of the human psyche unless you are, in fact, a Buddhist monk. While it is unrealistic to be in a state of presence at all times throughout the course of the day, we can make a habit of returning to presence throughout the day so we force ourselves to remember that whatever may have happened in the past has no ability to influence what will happen in the future unless we give it that ability.

Next time you find yourself needing to complete some activity to which you're currently averse, ask yourself why it is you dislike it so much. Is it inherently evil? It probably isn't. You probably just have an negative association with it due to past events which are currently prompting worse-case imaginings of the future.

Remember that fear is the emotion with the greatest influence on the human subconscious, so you're not only giving the past and future power over the present they don't actually have, you're likely doing so by exaggerating how often you've failed previously relative to how many times you've succeeded.

If we are able to stay present, we are able to consciously strip what has occurred in the past of the power to have any bearing on the present task at hand. We are able to treat each cold call (for example) as it actually is, an independent action the result of which is not dependent on anything other than what it is that you do *right now*.

How can we ensure we are able to regularly clear away the cobwebs of the past and terrible conjectures of the future so that we can focus on what must be done now? The answer, of course, is habit.

Creating a habitual inclination towards the present is why many people meditate to begin their day. By starting the morning in the state of presence meditation helps create, we can implore our minds to stay present throughout the course of the day.

And, before the practice of presence truly becomes a habit, we can schedule "presence breaks" throughout the day by setting the alarms on our phones for set times where we are forced to come back from wherever we are to the here and now.

Eventually we will need fewer reminders to return to presence and find ourselves doing so even when our alarm hasn't prompted us. This is an indication of presence taking up a larger share of our default state, and that's a good place to be.

It's a place where instead of putting activities off that we need to perform in order to reach our desired destination, we take action without thinking about them twice. It makes us much more efficient in carrying out every aspect of our sales process, and our lives.

3. Trust a Process

"Becoming is better than being." – Carol Dweck

"Fuck you, that's my name. You know why, mister? 'Cause you drove a Hyundai to get here tonight and I drove an $80,000 BMW. That's my name. And your name is 'you're wanting,' and you can't play in the man's game. You can't close them. And you go home and tell your wife your troubles. Because only one thing counts in this life. Get them to sign on the line which is dotted. You hear me? A-B-C. A – Always, B- Be, C-Closing, Always Be Closing, ALWAYS Be Closing!"

This scene from *Glengarry Glen Ross* is legendary, but the, uh, advice Alec Baldwin's character gives to a group of struggling sales reps to "always be closing" is pretty worthless.

Closing isn't a single action and, therefore, it is not something we can "always" be doing. Rather, closing is the result of a holistic set of actions, executed consistently. Closing is a process. To become a closer it is therefore important to become more process-oriented.

A focus on optimizing process, coupled with consistency in the execution of the individual elements that comprise that process, are what make the results inevitable.

It's a focus that's closely correlated with the just-discussed ability to operate from the present, because by executing the current step in your process necessitates your focus be on whatever needs to be done right now.

The opposite occurs when we focus on results, as the gap between where we are vs. where we want to be (e.g. as a % of our quota) has us spending our time stressing and procrastinating instead.

Most of us in sales set pretty audacious goals, or we have lofty goals set for us by senior leadership. This can make us feel like we're under a lot of pressure, particularly when a few months of the sales year have gone by and we still haven't closed anything. If we're not careful, the pressure we feel will eventually turn into fear as future nightmare scenarios now seem like legitimate possibilities. That fear has the potential to manifest in two ways.

The first way it might manifest is by having us second guess everything that we've been doing to this point. Doubt in how we conduct our sales activities generally leads to analysis paralysis, where we're so busy second guessing ourselves as to whether we're doing the right things that we don't end up doing much of anything at all. Now we definitely aren't going to hit our goals.

The second way this fear can manifest is by inducing us to work harder, but less intelligently. As time passes and we're still without that first deal, we abandon our well-thought out strategic approach and start sending out mass emails to every prospect we have. The quality of our meetings suffers as the people who have time to respond to this kind of sales spam are the type of people that just like to talk, kick tires, or both. They are not the sort of prospect most inclined to help us win the 2nd Sale discussed earlier. They are the opposite.

The sales culture at your company probably doesn't help here. Most sales organizations rank reps based on year-to-date performance and then publish these rankings for everyone to see, often hanging them all over the office walls.

While this is generally justified on the basis of sales reps being people "who love to compete," in reality it's a calculated tactic your company knows will spur you to work harder. And, much like the reason your company implements a basic, watered down sales methodology across the sales floor, it does this because it's more practical to get reps to throw shit at the wall consistently than it is for them to genuinely invest in each rep's ability to become a closer.

Instilling a sense of fear that you're going to fail if you don't work harder at the very least gets mediocre reps to put in the work. Fear is our greatest motivator, after all, and your company as a corporate entity is in all likelihood not going to care how many extra hours of work it takes you to produce results so long as it hits its revenue targets for the quarter.

It is important for the closer to keep a vigilant focus on process even if their company is screaming "results, motherfucker!" because it is the careful refinement of the individual pieces of your process that will inevitably lead you to achieve results even greater than what management is trying to get out of you in the first place. Giving into the urge to start working harder but less strategically will only make you less likely to achieve them.

Now, just because you should trust in process doesn't mean you should necessarily trust *your* process as it currently stands. Like the closer's ability to treat sales activities as a game of chess by becoming habitually aware of the all moves she could make vs. the one she should, so too does the closer habitually reevaluate their process to see which areas could be better systemized to produce more results over less time spent.

This is especially critical in the would-be closer's early stages of development, as we naturally lean towards a particular way of doing things that might not make any sense at all. The sooner the closer can expose the ineffective aspects of their process, the sooner they can make improvements to them.

Once these improvements are made and results start coming in the form of closed deals, the closer should continue to reevaluate their process periodically. However, you should be guarded against making any changes unless you are certain those changes would be an upgrade over how you currently do things.

After all, there will always be another way to do something, but we can't discount the idea that maybe the way we do things is already good enough. This idea is corroborated by Parkinson's Law.

4. Pray to Parkinson

"The best is the enemy of the good." – Voltaire

Early on in my sales career I put together what I thought was the world's best business case for my prospect to put in front of his CEO. It was comprised of a PowerPoint some 30+ slides that explained the ins and outs of my company's value proposition to the prospect organization to a level of specificity that left no question or concern unaddressed.

I had gone into great detail about how everyone on the prospect's team was going to benefit from the agreement, including those who had not been present for any of our meetings. I even made the PowerPoint easily navigable by creating links between the pages so that my prospect and his CEO would be able to hop around the gargantuan deck without getting lost.

My prospect's meeting with his CEO wasn't for another week after I had presented him with pricing, and I gave myself the entirety of that time to work on the business case.

Subconsciously I told myself it was vitally important to put together something killer, and I felt lucky to have so much time to work on it. I proceeded by taking an hour or so each day until the day before I would send it to my prospect, when I spent a whopping 6 hours combing over every final detail to make sure it was absolutely perfect.

As soon as I sent it to my prospect I got a prompt response from him that read "Joe, there's way too much detail in here. I need this to be about 10x shorter."

Parkinson's Law is the idea that "work expands so as to fill the time available for its completion."

This means that if we give ourselves a week to complete a task, we will take that entire week to complete that task even if we could do a good enough job in a day.

Our subconscious will find reasons for not doing things more quickly, nitpicking at inconsequential aspects of the task and letting the perfect become the enemy of the good just as our dude Voltaire had warned.

In the example above, I had actually known that my prospect was a "less is more" kind of guy, but given all the time I had to create the proposal I convinced myself that it was better to go over the top anyway.

It is important to be cognizant of Parkinson's Law at every step in carrying out the individual elements of our sales process. We must incline ourselves towards allowing too little time to get a task done rather than too much. In giving ourselves only enough time to complete a task that it makes us sweat a little, we will be forced to focus only on what is absolutely necessary.

The effect of this practice is to make us much more efficient with the deals we have in play, creating more time for us to spend meeting with additional prospects we wouldn't get to otherwise. In fact, if you could become really good at never succumbing to Parkinson's Law, you'd likely double up your peers in terms of deals closed just by being able to take so many more meetings than them.

If you have a proposal due to a client in a week, don't allow yourself the whole week to complete it. Block out one hour on whichever day makes the most sense and work on it only for that hour. If it still needs more work afterwards, block out another 15 minutes, but do whatever you can not to keep dragging it out indefinitely, or the next thing you know you'll have spent your entire week on something that was good enough a few days ago.

5. Some Like it Hard

"It's supposed to be hard. If it wasn't hard, everyone would do it. The hard is what makes it great." - Tom Hanks as Jimmy Dugan, A League of Their Own

This is the line of thinking that saved me from abandoning my sales career before it ever got off the ground. It was a light in the dark when I just didn't feel I had the energy to shake off another lost deal and focus on the next one instead. It was that which propelled me to pick up the phone one more time after everyone else had left the office for the evening.

Becoming a closer is not a cake walk and, true to the quote, everyone would become one if it were. I mean, what person works in finance as an accountant making $60k a year when their friends a few rows over in sales are raking in over six figures? A real sicko, that's who.

There is a certain amount of safety in most office jobs that don't fall under the purview of "sales." It's the safety of not having a Medusa waiting on the other end of the phone to turn you into stone for having the audacity to call her unexpectedly. It's the safety of not having to deal with people telling you "no" over and over to the point where you start believing you're professionally inept. It's the safety of not having your inability to do the job well displayed for your whole company to see when it ranks its reps based on performance. Sales is hard and becoming a closer is harder. But that's what makes it great.

During the first few pages of this book I said there wouldn't be anything contained in these pages that would constitute a shortcut, and that implementing the ideas I've written about wouldn't be a cakewalk. I also said that the closer rejoices in that notion. This is because the closer understands that, because closing requires a lot of the type of effort most people don't want to expend, they improve their odds of success dramatically by merely continuing to execute when everyone else would let the despair of a lost deal prevent them from taking the action necessary to set the next meeting. Those people never get to the "tipping point" closers reach where all their efforts pay off.

And, because commission structures typically favor disproportionately those reps that are able to do significantly above what's expected, each difficulty the closer faces is a reminder that other people are lying down while they continue to climb. It's not hard to see why, then, the closer not only tolerates the difficult aspects of their job, they actually begin to look forward to these kicks to the teeth.

In this sense closers are like marathon runners, only we're marathon runners running a course where walls spring up from the ground and into the sky at random. These are all the "no's" we don't see coming and mental anguish we go through when mired in a slump. We're all going to hit these walls and fall down at some point, and most of us will hit a wall once or twice and have the ability to climb over it after licking our wounds a little bit first. Very few of us, however, are able to hit walls repeatedly and steadfastly climb over each one without thinking twice about it. Show me the rep that is able to this with a smile on their face and I'll show you a closer.

Next time you face what you've previously considered to be a crushing rejection, don't spend time ruminating on it, relish in it instead. In each failure is the opportunity for us to become more immune to that failure's negative effects. If failure loses the power to affect us, we will find it impossible to fail.

6. Learn & Live

"Self-education is, I firmly believe, the only kind of education there is." – Isaac Asimov

Until my mid-twenties I suffered from a common affliction the mind. It is a societal-borne affliction for which there are no PSAs, and one that isn't properly recognized for the epidemic it is. It is an affliction of helplessness. It is the misguided, erroneous, and silent assumption that once our formal education ends, so too does our need to keep learning.

During college we took a variety of classes with a wide range of applicability to the skills we'd need in real life. Although the usefulness of these classes depended in part on our chosen areas of study, on the whole our reliance on our formal education as the primary path to our success, however defined, appears now to have been misguided.

As a liberal arts major, for example, I feel comfortable saying the majority of what has attributed to any success I've had in my adult life is due in large part to the education I've given myself *after* I got my diploma.

My "post-education education" began after realizing that for all our years in school, we don't actually spend any time discussing what it actually means to learn, or how we might learn better than our current practices allow us. We almost never got direction in understanding how to take newly learned concepts and apply them to real world scenarios to produce desired outcomes. We were merely given information and told to remember it for an exam.

A love of lifelong education has produced some of the world's greatest minds. Elon Musk was bullied and spent the majority of his time as a child learning as a result, which eventually became a life-long passion. In his adult life, the amount of specialized knowledge he's accumulated and wielded in his business ventures has propelled him into the limelight as one of the world's greatest entrepreneurs. If Musk is unfamiliar to you, perhaps you've heard that Warren Buffett spends as much as 80% of his waking hours reading.

Why is it then, when we have abundant examples of those who have embraced a lifelong love of education going on to achieve extraordinary results, that so many of us cease our educational endeavors after college? Not only do many of us stop learning, we even go so far as to look down upon those that continue to do so in an effort to improve their lives. We call these people "try hards," as if what Thoreau said about conscious endeavor could be anything other than admirable.

The abandonment of our educational endeavors isn't entirely our fault. Our formative years were filled with society reinforcing the notion that success was akin to a packaged commodity available for purchase to anyone with a diploma from a "good" school and a decent GPA. We bit on the notion that checking these items off a list would open the right doors for us, then found ourselves not being able to find those doors in the first place once we hit the job market.

How many times have we heard stories about the single mother who, through extreme poverty and misfortune, managed to work three jobs so that her children could have the ability to go to college? Nobody mentions the harsh reality that all that mother's hard work could be for nothing if her children come out of college and can't make use of the diploma they've earned.

Moreover, many traditional institutions of higher learning are not equipped to prepare young adults for the Digital Era. The economic and societal shifts produced by the perpetually expanding adoption of digital technologies are rapidly changing the skills we need to compete. They're also creating an immense amount of opportunity for those that have them by all but eliminating traditional barriers to entry in every market.

And yet, most colleges and universities are staffed with professors teaching students as if the skills and subjects universities have traditionally taught are just as valuable today as they were during 1990s. How are colleges going to adapt when it becomes obvious that an investment of four years is better spent by an 18-year-old building out a massive social media following than by pursuing a degree in the humanities?

What all this means is that it is now more important than ever that we take our education into our own hands and vigorously keep up with the information and skills which give us the power to create opportunities for ourselves that didn't exist 20 years ago. The access to the information we need is ubiquitously available, and if we don't make a habit of putting it to use, the people who do will be the ones that snag the job instead of us, or the ones that are able to create opportunities for themselves that negate the need for a traditional job altogether.

An insidious and related consequence in the abandonment of our educations post-college is learned helplessness, whereby we're constantly looking for someone to show us the "right" way of doing things rather than using our own critical thinking and creativity to figure it out on our own.

Learned helplessness is a big reason so many people stay in careers they hate, feeling as though an opportunity must be presented in order for them to leave their current situation instead of proactively taking the actions needed to create the opportunity for themselves.

It's also important to understand that your sales organization may very well be apt to foster this sense of learned helplessness within you, even if it's not willful. A corporation, the profitability of which depends on keeping the costs of attracting, training and retaining talent manageable, has every reason to make their reps feel like "success" is something they can teach you to achieve, not something you create for yourself. Again, this isn't necessarily malevolent, it just is what it is.

In addition to embracing a lifelong commitment to learning how to better ourselves, we must also reorient the *way* we learn, as we've been conditioned to use ineffective learning techniques which constitute passive learning. We must make the shift to active learning instead, which in many instances means not only consuming information, but making sure to take action upon the information we've consumed to produce desired outcomes.

In developing the expertise to become compellingly relevant to our prospects, I detailed an active learning technique designed to make the critical information pertaining to our prospect's world more easily recallable during the heat of a prospect meeting. For other skills, active learning might mean physically taking a new idea and putting it into practice immediately such that it becomes muscle memory.

For those that are more familiar with my photography, this is how I learned to take professional level photographs over the matter of a couple months while I was selling for Gartner while traveling in Iceland, Amsterdam, and Italy.

I simply wouldn't read or watch a YouTube video pertaining to some photographic skill without simultaneously trying it out in real time. I found this to be much more effective than learning about the skill in question and then waiting until I found myself in the field to implement it, at which point I had difficulty remembering what I had "learned."

I mentioned Warren Buffet as an example of someone who has embraced a love of lifelong learning, and that he is rumored to spend about 80% of his day reading. I don't necessarily believe that. I believe it is far more likely that he spends something like 40% percent of his day reading and 40% of his day taking action based upon what he's learned. Whether this means investing in new companies based on the financial reports he's just pored over or whatever else, you don't become one of the world's wealthiest people by simply accumulating knowledge, but by taking action on the basis of that knowledge to manifest outcomes from it.

Closers should take care not to become victims of learned helplessness by waiting around to be told how to do their jobs. They should instead have the mentality that they're going to actively educate themselves to the point that no one would ever feel that were necessary.

"Of all the featherless beasts, only man, chained by his self-imposed slavery to the clock, denies the elemental fire and proceeds as best he can about his business, suffering quietly, martyr to his madness. Much to learn." – Edward Abbey

Part III: The Office Escape Manual

1. The Work-Life Lie

The silver bullet every recruiter has in their back pocket to lure the unsullied into the 1st round of interviews. A fabricated good life. A particularly pathetic zeitgeist of our generation. At its core a lie we buy into on behalf of our ego. The "work-life balance."

Balance suggests equality, and while I'm usually alright with math, I can't conjure up any equation where 5 days = 2 days.

Let's keep in a whole hundo for a minute. Any job that *requires* you to come to the office for 40+ hours a week does not give you anything close to a "balanced" life. Remember that, in addition to the hours spent in the office, you've got commute time, time spent stressing about quotas and after-hours emails that you don't *technically* need to respond to...but aren't you up for that promotion?

What's more, the time we consider "free" is by-in-large dictated by what we have going on at work, manifesting in innocuous-looking text messages that are really indications of anything but a life well-balanced:

"Sorry, gotta bail on dinner, really big presentation tomorrow."

"Hey, can you pick up the kids today? I'm gonna have to stay late at work trying to salvage this deal."

"Jim – I have to cancel my guitar lesson tonight. I have too much going on at work. We'll reschedule."

The more you analyze what exactly is entailed with working in an office environment full-time, the more conspicuous a crock of shit the purported work-life balance becomes. What's more, when we put it under the microscope, we can see what our acceptance of the work-life lie really is: a consolation prize for giving up on our individual potentials in exchange for a modest heaping of canned success.

This can be the only reason for why we accept such a blatant falsehood. It's simply a much more pleasant means to consider our reality than the alternative of acknowledging that we've settled for less than we're capable. More agonizingly, that by settling we've created a situation in which we'll never be able to explore the limits of our potentials.

Your employer understands the power inherent in enticing your ego to buy into the work-life lie. This doesn't mean that your CEO and the rest of the corporate oligarchy are bad people, it simply means that the incentives of a corporate entity when aggregated aren't always going to align with your own. In this instance, your employer is incentivized to create a workforce which buys into a generic version of "work-life balance" because such a workforce is stable and cost-effective.

By stressing the importance of the "balance" we are afforded as part of our employment, the inklings we have dancing in our peripheries to explore that which we've been daydreaming about since we were children, the oats we've had waiting patiently all of our lives to be sewn, start to seem foolish when we buy into the idea that what we want instead is something our employer is already providing us.

The prospect of leaving your employer turns from a feeling of foolishness to one of fear with the passage of time, as our skillset becomes more tailored to our employer and less tailored to the market as a whole. The safety of the status quo is exaggerated by our subconscious, which fills our head with images of people laughing at our failures.

What's more, if we buy into the work-life lie, we also buy into the notion that any hours we do have free and clear of our employment should be primarily spent on leisure and relaxation. Watching football. Sitting on the beach. Watching Netflix.

The thing is, if all we're doing with our time is coming into the office or relaxing, we don't have any time left to create the app we've dreamt up with our roommate. We don't have any time left to learn how to invest in stocks or real estate. We won't have any time left to allocate towards creating the type of life we've dreamt about ever since we were young. And so, by buying into the work-life lie and the lifestyle it connotes, we also buy into becoming life-long runners of the rat race.

In this sense, while it's true that an office environment can't truly provide us with a lifestyle one could consider "balanced," it's also erroneous to believe "balance" is something we should aspire to anyway.

Why would we aspire to "balance" instead of filling our lives with that which gives us the most fulfillment at the near exclusion of everything else?

Recall that I started this book pontificating about greatness, however you might define it for yourself. That one couldn't simply be great, but instead had to make a habit out of making choices between alternatives that were most likely to lead to great things.

I argued that this was a pragmatic and drama-free way of living. Pragmatic because, while we often glorify successful people and tout all the "sacrifices" they've made to achieve their success, orienting our decisions towards greatness simplifies our lives by giving us a compass always pointing towards our own version of magnetic north. Drama-free because it is less stressful than the way most of us live – in a perpetual state of uncertainty due to only halfway pursuing our dreams, always left wondering what we might accomplish instead of creating a lifestyle which guarantees us to find out.

I mention this again now because making the pragmatic choice of greatness often times necessitates the pragmatic decision to live a life with less balance, not more of it. That's because a "well-balanced" life typically connotes some canned version of what other people consider to be "normal," not necessarily that which we want for ourselves in terms of maximizing the things which bring us the most fulfillment and minimizing those which do not.

Bear in mind that just about anyone who's ever accomplished what they really wanted in life didn't structure their life around balance, or they wouldn't have allowed themselves the hours needed to accomplish whatever it was that ended up defining them. The greater the accomplishment, the greater the need for an almost singular focus taking up the vast majority of that person's time.

Many of us had something we were passionate about to this extent at one point in our lives, but we've traded it in for weekends spent on Netflix binges and watching other people play sports on Saturdays *and* Sundays. Often times we even laud ourselves for settling down. After all, if we had chased the version of our lives we really wanted when we were young, we wouldn't have had the opportunity to build the life of such exceptional balance we're leading now...

*

So what exactly am I advocating for here? I started by pointing out that there's no actual balance to current work-life scenarios, but that balance isn't something for which you should strive anyway. True and true.

However, it is one thing to tell you to orient all your time towards whatever it is that brings you the most fulfillment, that which defines your greatness, and another to be in the financial situation to where you can go after those dreams in earnest.

This is exactly why becoming a closer is uniquely awesome: it creates an environment where you can use the leverage you've created from your uncommon success on the sales floor to escape the office and create more time to go after whatever it is you want to define your greatness while still getting paid handsomely along the way.

To get to this point often means working *more* hours learning how to close deals than your company would ever dream of asking of you while still purporting to provide its employees "balance."

But only at first:

1. The additional hours you spend honing the skills outlined in the Sales Domination Manual, particularly to developing the acumen inherent in the Compelling Relevance trigger, are those that will bring your potential as a closer to fruition.

2. Becoming a closer is what comes with the ability to leverage your success to begin working outside the office on your own terms.

3. Once you've reached this point, you'll have such an acute understanding of how to close deals that it's akin to muscle memory, and since you've escaped the office, you can now reallocate much of your time towards whatever lights your soul on fire while still making 6 figures as a young deal god.

"Balance" doesn't have any place in getting you to this point. "Balance" has you coming into the office 8-9 hours a day until you're 70 instead.

2. You've Been Trained...For Sales Mediocrity

Your company's goal is to maximize profits, either for shareholders or investors in some other capacity (e.g. private equity), and those who benefit disproportionately from the profitability of the organization sit at the top of its org chart, i.e. not you and not likely to be you unless you are willing to dedicate a good portion of your life to slogging your way through corporate serfdom.

I am not asserting this is a bad thing – I am very glad to live in a society where someone can roll up their sleeves and become the CEO of a company. And, although your CEO and other members of the corporate oligarchy benefit disproportionately to their workers in regards to the success of the company, they are providing you the means to sell a product without incurring any of the overhead you would as an entrepreneur. This is merely a reminder that you should always consider whether your company's incentives are also your own, and a behest to stay woke in light of these considerations.

The employer-employee misalignment of incentives can be seen when considering the motives behind your company's sales methodology.

As a profit-driven entity, your company relies on consistently generating revenues and keeping costs down. To that end, your company chooses to have its sales floor sell via a canned selling methodology because it's something the average rep can follow, and therefore it leads to consistent, predictable results across the sales floor while keeping sales training costs to a sustainable level.

In other words, your company's MO is not to recognize the personal ceiling of each of its individual reps. That would require intolerably more expense and training time when there's no guarantee that reps would make sufficient use out of all the additional training to make it worthwhile.

What's more, as your company grows, the incentive to implement a dumbed-down version of what it takes to close deals only increases as it finds itself requiring something that can be scaled across an increasing influx of new hires, getting them on the sales floor quickly.

Contrast this highly efficient means of training new hires vs. the amount of resources it would take to capitalize upon each new rep's individual potential as a closer when, in your company's defense, there is no assurance that the new rep in question has any real inclination to become a closer in the first place. Again, the difference in expense would be immense.

What's more, using a silver-bullet sales methodology helps instill confidence in the many reps who have no real desire to become closers in the first place and would otherwise be lost as soon as they picked up the phone.

It tells these reps that it is still possible to close deals so long as they throw enough shit at the wall such that some of it eventually sticks. And so the vast majority of reps do just that and close a few deals over the course of the year, to the satisfaction of their company for which this was the plan all along, and to the disappointment of the individual rep who's left confused as to why they've achieved only mediocre results when they had so steadfastly followed a selling methodology which had promised them more.

Finally, there's recruitment efforts to consider. Much like the peddling of the Work-Life Lie, which has the effect of making young people believe what they want is a bunch of full-time work weeks until they retire, the evangelization of a sales methodology helps recruiters reach out to young adults with no sales experience on the basis that their sales training academy will "teach them everything they need to know" about closing deals.

The promotion and teaching of a canned sales methodology like *Value Selling* is a convenient way to hide the truth: That to be really good at closing new business, you're going to at first have to work much harder and more strategically than the average sales rep to develop the skills outlined in the Sales Domination Manual to get to that point.

"Yes, you can make money here, but it will require more work than most people your age are willing to put in" isn't a line that plays well if you're a corporate recruiter tasked with redirecting young talent from the classroom to the office in droves.

You can witness how predictable, scalable sales results are more important to your company than the development of individual closing ability in the form of the metrics your sales organization uses to track rep activity.

Anyone who's been in sales for any significant period of time has dealt with the frustration of having to track sales-related activity in some capacity. At the lowest level, some sales organizations still make their reps track how many cold calls they make to prospects on a daily basis. #Yeesh.

Even sales organizations that don't go full *Boiler Room* on their reps in this regard at the very least make them track things like discovery calls or new deal opportunities on a week over week basis.

Forcing reps to track and log their activity is this manner has a net positive effect on mediocre sales reps who need the poking and prodding just to show up every day. There is a surprising amount of reps that fall into this boat, and for these reps keeping track of their sales activity at least gets them on the phones and in prospect inboxes when there's no guarantee they would do so much otherwise.

It has a net negative impact on would-be closers, however, who would be better served by taking the time to strategically approach their sales year by reaching out to their best prospects after they've begun developing the skills outlined in the Sales Domination Manual with messaging strategically designed to begin establishing the right Mental Triggers in their prospects' minds from their very first outreach.

With a metrics-based focus forcing reps to start prospecting as soon as the calendar hits 1/1, would-be closers are not able to take the time to tailor their messaging, and they thereby begin to erode their ability to establish the Mental Triggers before they've even had the chance to speak with the prospect, who is now only sold on the idea of *not* doing that.

The consequences of this cannot be understated. If your communications signal to the prospect that you're an average, time-wasting sales parrot that doesn't really understand their world, it will be very hard to get their subconscious to ever see you as the type of person that warrants their time. The result is that you end up in the SPAM folder of both inbox and mind.

Most troubling, by forcing reps to track things like discovery meetings per week, management is signaling to reps that what's important is the activity itself, not what the activity is intended to produce. This tells would-be closers they should value quantitative actions over the qualitative actions. I hope this lights a fire under your ass, because what this also signals is a vote of "no confidence" in terms of you being able to sell strategically based on your own critical thinking ability.

Again, the lesson from all this is not to start viewing your employer as some inherently evil entity, but to recognize how its incentives differ from your own in various instances which can actually serve to limit your potential as a closer, not develop it. It is important to remain aware of this so that the decisions you make on your path to becoming a closer and escaping the office are oriented towards your own incentives.

One of the primary benefits of escaping the office and beginning to work on your own terms is that you won't have to put up with an undue degree of micromanagement any longer. In the interim, it is critical that if you are obligated to hit a certain amount of quantitative metrics each week that the activity used to satisfy these metrics is targeted at your lower-tier prospect organizations.

This might equate to setting some meetings which don't have a chance of going anywhere, but the effect is to insulate your "must-win" prospects from the sort of indiscriminate messaging that could get you shut out before you even have the chance to meet with them.

3. The Office, The Thief

As it turns out, not only does your sales organization end up training you for sales mediocrity as a new hire, you're then thrust into an environment that makes any alternative all but impossible if you're not properly attuned to it.

As alluded to in "A Day in the Doldrums," there are simply too many distractions competing for our attention in an office environment for us to truly be productive with the 8-9 hours we're there each day. Too many meetings which have nothing to do with closing new business, too many office fantasy football leagues, too many theoretical promotions for positions that deep down we don't even want.

As the digital era unfolds, our collective attention span is hardly up to the task of ignoring all the dank memes on your Instagram feed, let alone your buddy coming over from a few rows down and having you look at them when you've resisted the temptation on your own.

Things are so bad, in fact, that Inc. Magazine has found that we only spend 2 hours and 53 minutes actually working while we're in the office each 8-hour workday. Yikes.

Why, oh God, would the majority of enterprises force their employees to be in the office for so much time in which they're not directly contributing to any tangible business outcome? Wouldn't it be better for employees if we were able to use the time we aren't actually working to better ourselves in some other capacity?

That's a rhetorical question, of course. It would certainly be better for us as individual employees. The thing is, young closer, for your employer these hours aren't wasted at all.

That's because it is in part the sheer number of hours spent in the office that create the company lifers your employer relies upon to ensure the ongoing financial viability of the organization as a whole. Employee churn is a huge expense for all corporate entities, and it's especially high in sales due to turnover caused by burnout.

In keeping tabs on you by literally *keeping* you, your employer creates the conditions where they can serve up the company Kool-Aid all. day. long. It's the Kool-Aid that reinforces the Work-Life Lie and tells employees they are fortunate to be a part of their company's success.

After all, if you were left to your own devices, if you weren't in an environment where you were forced to be *at work* for 8-9 hours to produce 3 hours' worth *of work*, who knows what you might do with all your newly re-acquired time? You might very well leave the company altogether when, not surrounded by Bobs, you decide to pursue something else entirely. That wouldn't be very cost-effective.

All this is a damn shame too, because most reps don't have any sort of inkling like this; they just don't want to come to the cube-farm every day, especially when they're not actually working for over half the time they're there.

In fact, many reps' individual results would stand to benefit significantly from working from outside company confines because they would no longer be subjected to all the distractions inherent to an office environment, thereby allowing them to work in whatever manner they're most efficient.

In the end, any potential benefits to individual rep performance are trumped by the value to your company of creating lifelong worker bees directly under its control. This is why you must take the success that warrants your office exodus into your own hands. No one else at your organization is going to do it for you.

4. Flying the Coop

When, where, and how you work. When you've
established yourself as a closer, these are yours to decide.
Your employer won't let you fly the coop on the basis of
gratitude alone (although that will likely be a factor), but for
the same reasons it implements a dumbed-down sales
methodology and keeps its employees at the office in the first
place: risk and expense.

On the micro level, the most obvious risk of course is that
you walk away because your employer refuses to grant you
the autonomy to carry out your responsibilities whilst out
from underneath its watchful eye. The bigger, less obvious
risks go beyond losing you and your propensity to close deals
to another company, however.

For senior leadership, the bigger risks are reputational; the
risk of egg on the face if, rather than retaining top talent as

the company mandate requires, they start losing their top closers instead.

As you will see, by way of your uncommon success on the sales floor you'll become something of a poster child for your sales organization as a whole, even if by this point you are blatantly approaching how you close business much more strategically than what your company's selling methodology mandates. In this capacity your senior leadership team is likely to rely upon you as a source of morale for struggling reps yet to see results.

The poster child deciding there are greener pastures elsewhere is never a good look, particularly when considering the impact on inexperienced reps that may be easily influenced by the actions of more tenured reps. It's also a particularly bad look if the sales floor as a whole is struggling and you have been one of the lone bright spots to which your senior leadership team can point as proof that selling whatever it is that your company provides its customers isn't an impossible feat.

Your senior leadership team will in all likelihood allow you to escape the office based on these risks alone given the track record you'll establish by following the principles outlined in the Sales Domination Manual.

If you've taken your senior leadership team by surprise in making this request, or you're the first to lay out your office exodus as requisite to your continued employment with the company, your senior leadership team might be tempted to believe that in allowing you to work remote you'll prompt a lot of unqualified reps to demand the same. It would behoove you in this case to remind them that the ability to dictate how you work can be used to motivate reps to achieve results similar to your own.

It's a reward, not a right.

You may also want to have a good understanding of just how much it's going to cost to replace you if your employer were to let you walk. For each rep lost, your company is going to incur expenses it wouldn't have had if you had stayed, which run the gamut from hard costs to opportunity costs:

1) Recruiting and hiring a replacement
2) Putting that replacement through training
3) Getting that person to a place where they are consistently performing
4) Getting that person to a place where they are consistently performing to your level

While the rep that replaces you is still mired somewhere between stages 1-3 above, your employer has lost out on all the sales you could have closed in the interim, as well as the immeasurable costs to employee morale when the rest of the sales floor sees that one of its best closers believes she will be able to do better outside of company confines.

The stronger a closer you are, the more poignant these expenses would appear if you were to really make your way towards the exit.

In going over all of this, you might think I'm advocating for you, once you've built up the requisite leverage to justify leaving the office through a track record of sales dominance, to put the above together in a neat and tidy business case for office exodus you can then present to your manager and/or senior leadership team.

I'm not.

These are simply the facts you'll want to have in mind if your employer inconceivably starts to hem and haw once you inform them of your decision to vacate Club Fluorescent.

To their credit, mine didn't, and chances are if you've become the type of closer the Sales Domination Manual implores you to become, yours won't either.

5. Traveling the World While You Work

The gladdest moment in human life, me thinks, is a departure into unknown lands" – Sir Richard Burton

If you follow me on Instagram, you know my handle is @joey.views, but you might not know that it's a play on the nickname I earned during my tenure with Gartner, Joey Deals. It was the deals that enabled me to go after the views you see on my feed in the first place, and while the previous chapters entail the philosophy to closing new business that got me to that position, this chapter briefly goes over some things to consider if you decide like I did that what you want to do once you escape the office is travel the world while still holding down your 6-figure sales gig.

It's Easier Now Than Ever

It might behoove you to know that if this is something you want to pursue but have previously been put off by all the logistics that would seem to go into it, you've grossly overestimated how difficult it is to travel while working in the Digital Era.

For example, when people would ask how to reach me while abroad, most seemed surprised when I'd tell them just to him me on my regular ol' phone number, fam. That's because it's no longer impossible to go to a foreign country and use your phone like you would at home without getting destroyed on roaming charges.

For example, both ATT & Verizon have programs that allow you to use your phone internationally in the same capacity you would at home (say, with unlimited phone calls, messages, and data) for $10 per day. This means an end to the incredibly exorbitant roaming charges you might otherwise accumulate in setting yourself up to stay connected not matter where you are.

And, because you can use your smartphone as a hotspot through that same service provider, you now have both your laptop and smartphone available to you wherever you are to do business. If you've got a plan with unlimited data, this is huge, as it essentially gives you everything you need to close a deal in two objects for $10 a day. Invest in a good power bank, and if you plan on traveling by vehicle, a power inverter, which allows you to plug your 110v laptop into your rental car's 12v outlet to cap things off.

Now that you're able to stay connected so easily, you don't need to always take such care to plan around where you will and won't be able to get work done. You also minimize how important it is for your hotel/AirBnB to provide you with a reliable internet connection to stay connected to your prospects.

Granted, the strength of your service provider's network in the particular area of the world you will be traveling does play a role in just how much freedom you'll have, but both AT&T and Verizon offer data and voice maps on their websites that show you exactly where you're covered and where things might be too much of a toss-up.

Just a couple of years ago this level of connectivity wasn't possible by any practical measure, and it's a level of connectivity which makes the world small enough to be able to fully embrace a life of travel while still having the job security and pay that come with being a closer.

If you *do* find yourself in an area where you're lacking for internet access from your smartphone's network provider, then it will be vital you have reliable access to the internet in some other capacity to ensure you're still able to conduct business.

There are a few options here:

1) Most car rental companies offer an optional wifi adapter to be included with your rental. This allows you to tap into the network of a local service provider, and as an added benefit, you don't have to keep it in your car.

In fact, when I was in Italy in 2017, I got one of these adapters with my rental car and kept it in my backpack so I had reliable internet access whenever I would decide to plop down at some cafe to get work done. It is advisable to go this route over relying on coffee shops and bars themselves for internet access. Depending on where you are, "free wifi" at a cafe might mean something akin to dial-up speed. Besides, mobile internet is tops because you can't beat sitting in a Land Rover in northern Iceland, volcanic activity happening directly ahead of you, while simultaneously meeting with a prospect located in Pennsylvania.

2) If you need to rely on your hotel or Airbnb for internet access, bear in mind that wifi speeds are going to vary significantly, the importance of which depends on what sort of selling you do.

At Gartner the deals I closed were the product of a lot of meetings conducted over WebEx, which allowed me to share my screen and the presentation materials on it with prospects. To be able to do this consistently required a pretty fast internet connection. After getting burned once or twice I came to understand a few things about what I could expect from various types of accommodations:

   i) Four and five-star hotels are typically going to provide a solid internet connection with enough juice to get the job done. Anything less and it's 50/50, with some hotels providing "free wifi" in name only. This is a shame too, because there are plenty of mom & pop hotels out there that are clean and comfortable but lack in this one essential aspect of being able to get work done while abroad. If you haven't made it rain to the extent that you're comfortable staying in 4 and 5-star hotels wherever you travel, you'll want to call ahead to ensure a proper internet connection before booking with whatever hotel you're considering or opt instead for my preferred accommodations provider of choice, Airbnb.

   ii) Airbnb allows you to show only those homes where the internet is going to be of a certain echelon by enabling the "Business Essentials" filter. I have never had a problem staying connected while staying at a place that qualified for this label, and it's the first filter I apply when I'm looking to get work done while traveling.

If I decide I want to stay at a place that doesn't qualify for the "Business Essentials" filter, I'll usually message the Airbnb host before booking to confirm the reliability of the internet connection as a prerequisite to booking. As the profitability of their Airbnb establishment relies on the positive reviews they receive from guests, your host isn't going to lie to you if that's not the case.

Believe it or not, ensuring you'll have phone and internet access as we've done above is all that it takes to ensure you *can* work abroad, because what else besides your phone and the internet do you need to close a deal? The answer for most closers is "nothing." However, that's not it as far as it goes in regards to the practical realities of closing a prospect sitting in an office in New York from your Airbnb located, say, above the rice terraces of Sapa, Vietnam:

1) <u>Some time zones offer unique closing challenges</u> - this is one of the greatest realities you must account for when deciding where you want to travel. Sapa is 11 hours ahead of Eastern Time, and 14 ahead of Pacific Time, for example.

    This means that when you're setting a meeting with your prospect in New York and they suggest 3pm, you'll have to be prepared for how to respond (unless you're cool taking a meeting at 2am in the morning, you sicko). Traveling in countries that fall into time zones this far removed from that of your prospects means you'll have to take meetings at some very bizarre hours, like 7pm-midnight (8am-1pm on the east coast). If this isn't something you're prepared to do, you'll have to limit yourself in regard to which countries you travel. That isn't necessarily a bad thing, however, because...

2) <u>Some time zones offer unique closing advantages</u> - say that you're back in Iceland now instead of Vietnam. Iceland is only 5 hours ahead of New York, so the hours your prospects are typically going to be able to take meetings will between 1pm-10pm local time. When I was in Iceland I didn't want to take meetings after 5pm, so that meant that I'd schedule all of my meetings for 1pm-5pm (8am-12pm eastern). This gives you a couple of unique advantages you wouldn't have if you were in the same time zone as your prospect:

    i.   You'll never be unprepared for a meeting because you've been awake for several hours by the time your meeting rolls around. You can basically remove any possibility of you dropping the ball out of the equation altogether, unless you're one serious ball-dropping motherfucker.

    ii.   You help further establish the right Mental Triggers in the mind of your prospect, because while you're sending them follow up emails at 11am local time, they think you're sending them at 6am. This is a good thing particularly for the Reciprocity and Consistency Triggers, as their subconscious will urge them be equally as on the ball as the young deal god with whom they're working.

    iii.   You're able to schedule meetings only at times when you're in a natural state of "flow."

Flow is the state we're in when accomplishing tasks comes easily to us.

Conversely, when we're out of flow, even sending a simple email can become arduous. This is yet another reason it's a killer to *have* to work at the same times as everyone else by being forced to come into the office every day. What if I'm a night owl and my best work, because it's when I'm in flow, occurs from the hours of 8-midnight? Most of us would not say we're morning people, so if you're working from a country that's 5-6 hours ahead, you increase your productivity by not doing your most important work during a time of day when you're still clearing away the cobwebs.

3) <u>Certain geographic areas offer unique financial advantages</u> – working from certain countries gives you the ability to use the local currency to your advantage. Earn and dollars, spend and pesos, see which way your bank (account) goes.

4) <u>You won't be able to meet with prospects on site</u> - this may or may not be a disadvantage. You may have prospects that want to meet with you face to face or think that it will increase the likelihood of getting the deal closed when you've reached the 2nd sale. But for every one of these prospects, there is another prospect you visit in-house and accomplish nothing you couldn't have accomplished by teleconference. With these prospects all you've really done is wasted hours you could have allocated elsewhere, so it's really a wash in terms of the impact this could have on your overall ability to close deals while traveling.

Setting yourself up for perpetual travel

A lot of people don't end up pursuing their work-from-abroad dream because they can't mentally adjust to the idea of living as fluidly as a life of perpetual travel necessitates. This is also true if they like the idea of the lifestyle but don't set themselves up in a manner where they can actually embrace it.

Setting yourself up to be capable of living as a fluidly as a lifestyle of perpetual travel connotes requires that you rid yourself of your anchors, physical and emotional, that prevent you from fully embracing the incredible experiences you will otherwise have getting paid handsomely while you travel the world.

Our Stuff -One of the most salient of these anchors is all the stuff we own. If I'm going to work abroad indefinitely, what am I going to do with all of my stuff? Put it in storage? Sell it? My advice would be to just get rid of it. Keep what is of high personal importance to you and give everything else to your friends and Goodwill.

Embrace minimalism, not necessarily as some deep philosophical stance, but as practical solution to how difficult it can be to move around the world freely in body and mind if you aren't fully untethered. By keeping all of your stuff in storage somewhere, you're telling your subconscious that your "real" life is merely on hold. This, of course, has the effect of taking you out of the present and can prevent you from being open to everything that comes your way.

Additionally, you want to disassociate yourself from the type of person that cares about physical possessions more than experiences. You want to convey to yourself instead that you are the type of person who can have it all but need none of it.

The development of this belief is important because at some point in your life you will hit a speed bump in the road somewhere that you didn't see coming and you must be able to view your bounce back as a given. By placing so much importance on material possessions, we tell ourselves the opposite. We tell ourselves we are lucky to own what we have, and that we better hold onto all of it dearly, because who knows if we'd be able to get it back?

Significant (B)others - It goes without saying that if you're in a rocky relationship, or a relationship you're in just for the sake of being in a relationship, you're gonna have to drop it like it's hot. If you are truly in love with your SO then this obviously doesn't apply, but that person will have to come with you or you're liable to spend all your time abroad wishing they were there or end up buying a plane ticket home early.

Retaining residency at home - This is specific to young closers who have yet to buy a permanent residence. While it's true that you'll want to set yourself up to live fluidly by untethering yourself as much as possible, you'll still want to be *officially* tethered, as in retaining residency back home. You'll want to have an address you can use for a whole host of practical purposes, and while you might be able to use your parents' home address, or a friend's, it makes much more sense to get a virtual mailbox.

A virtual mailbox is a digitalized mailbox, a PO box designed for the Digital Era. It allows you to see what's in your mail when it's received wherever your mailbox is located, and for your provider to perform things like mail forwarding, recycling, and shredding according to your wishes. Most importantly, it gives you a virtual place to hang your hat for any entrepreneurial activities you may undertake once you've flown the coop and have thus created the time to pursue them.

6. Tomorrow Never Comes

You've reached the end of the book, and if I've done my job properly, you've sold yourself on committing to the type of closer you know you can become. The type of closer that earns double what they're expected to earn. The type of closer that can dictate where, when and how they work. The type of closer that can get an agreement signed from a prospect in LA while sitting at a rooftop bar in Dubai. The type of closer that can parlay an uncommon level of success on the sales floor into an employment situation where they have the time to invest in whatever it is that brings them the most fulfillment and whatever they choose to define their individual version of greatness.

It's a fantastic feeling, but it's a temporary one, and you must remember that this book has actually been nothing but a waste of your time if you don't take any action from it!

Don't wait until tomorrow to start implementing changes you can make today. Tomorrow never comes. There's too much time between now and then, too much risk that you'll get distracted, and with each day that passes you are less and less likely to take any action at all.

Remember, consistently closing new business is hard, and closers make a habit out of embracing the hard because they know it is the hard which takes others out of the game while they continue to play. Well, reading a book is easy, but taking immediate action from what you've read is not. Rejoice in this notion then, young closer, for you are one of the few that will decide to take action from what you've learned here right away, and as such you'll have made the choice most inclined towards your greatness.

ABOUT THE AUTHOR

Joe Duval took his first B2B entry-level sales position in late 2013 out of financial necessity. By 2017 he had leveraged his success as the top new business rep within his sales region two years in a row to travel the world while he worked, earning a promotion to a $200k/yr. enterprise position before leaving to write #ClosingSZN in an effort to help young professionals achieve their potentials as closers in order to create lifestyles in which they have more hours in the day to spend pursuing whatever it is that lights their souls on fire. He is also a photographer and creative whose work can be seen on Instagram @joey.views

You can also keep up with him @

www.joeduval.com

Made in the USA
Middletown, DE
19 November 2018